# Ekklesia . . .

## To The Roots Of Biblical Church Life

### Edited By
### STEVE ATKERSON

#### Contributors

BRIAN ANDERSON     JONATHAN LINDVALL

STEVE ATKERSON     TIM MELVIN

BILL GRIMES     HAL MILLER

BERESFORD JOB     DAN TROTTER

DAVID JOHN  ENS

D1413164

Special thanks to Christian Hidalgo of Navigation Advertising
for art direction and design.
www.navertise.com   christian@navertise.com
Ph 615-898-1496

*New Testament Restoration Foundation*
Atlanta, Georgia
**WWW.NTRF.ORG**

# Ekklesia . . .

## TO THE ROOTS OF BIBLICAL CHURCH LIFE

PUBLISHED BY
*New Testament Restoration Foundation*
2752 Evans Dale Circle
Atlanta, GA  30340  USA
WWW.NTRF.ORG

February, 2003

ISBN 0-9729082-0-X

To my wife, Sandy, who stood faithfully by me during my ecclesiological pilgrimage, to my late dad, Tommy, whose vision and support made this book possible, and to my step-mom, Lucie, for her help and interest in seeing God's Word spread throughout the world.

new testament
restoration
foundation

# TABLE OF CONTENTS

God, in His providence, has shown us some areas of church practice that we believe have been neglected. We are persuaded that a return to the way the original apostles did things could bring a tremendous blessing to the Bride of Christ. Those of us who participated in the writing of this book have enjoyed these blessings for years, and desire very much to see all who belong to Jesus feast at the banquet along with us.

While we are firmly convinced that God's best is for all His people to organize their churches according to NT patterns, we are not "against" everyone else. What we are against is divisiveness or the blanket condemnation of our brothers who see things differently than we do. Our desire is not to come across as judgmental or overly critical. Matters of church practice are much in the same category as the issue of believer's baptism verses infant baptism. People of faith can be found in each camp. Assuming that the Lord prefers one approach over the other, then the other method is "wrong." Is the wrong group therefore in sin? Are they thus not a true church? Will God refuse to work in and through them? Heaven forbid! While they may be in violation of God's best, it is an honest, sincere blunder in a completely different category than moral failings such as lying, theft, murder, rebellion, etc. We understand that sincere, Godly saints see the same Scripture passages differently. As Paul asked, "Who are you to judge someone else's servant? To his own master he stands or falls. And he will stand, for the Lord is able to make him stand" (Ro 14:4).

We advocate orthodox, historic, classic Christianity poured into the wineskin of New Testament church practice as established by the apostles. Thus, what we advocate herein concerns ortho*praxy* (right behavior), rather than ortho*doxy* (right theology). Our goal is to be Christ honoring and thoroughly biblical in every area concerning our church life. Thus, in the pages that follow, we argue strongly from Scripture for such things as living room sized churches, the Lord's Supper as a full meal, church leaders as servants (rather than lords), government by consensus, the right and responsibility of the brothers to make decisions corporately, no clergy-laity distinction, and interactive (participatory) church meetings. As you can see from the above, just because we advocate a home-based, relational, family-styled church does not mean that careful attention to order and organization are unimportant.

Some believers will occasionally object, "All that really matters is that we love Jesus, right?" Loving Jesus is indeed the central issue. However, Jesus Himself insisted that those who do love Him will "obey what I command . . . whoever has my commands and obeys them, he is the one who loves Me" (Jn 14:15-21). To listen to the voice of Christ, as Head of His church and the Captain of our souls, is of utmost importance. Jesus had some specific commands about His church. Thus we see that it takes both the wine and the wine skin, both the precept and the pattern. Without dispute the wine skin exists for the sake of the wine, but without the skin the wine spills to the ground and is wasted. It is a false dichotomy to hold to either one without the other. Attention to detail is needed.

We respectfully present this book to the church at large for consideration. It is the result of both years of study and day to day practical experience. We simply ask that you search the Scriptures as did the Bereans to see if these things be so. This entire study of the church is only a stepping stone to put us in a position of better being all Christ wants us to be as His body of people. May the Lord be pleased to grant all His people an ever deeper knowledge of Himself and His Bride!

— Stephen E. Atkerson, Editor

new testament
restoration
foundation

# Part I
## CHURCH MEETINGS

# 1
## APOSTOLIC TRADITION: OBSOLETE?

Suppose a newly planted, first century church in Alexandria, Egypt wrote a letter to the apostles over in Jerusalem. Imagine that this church is made up of Jewish believers who heard the gospel on a visit to Jerusalem, and then went back home to Alexandria. Now that they were back home, they didn't quite know what do to next. So, in this letter to the apostles was a series of questions about church life:

"Dear Apostles . . .

Why is it that we meet together as God's people?

What should we do in our meetings?

How often should we meet? Every Sabbath?

Does it matter where we meet?

Should we build a temple like in Jerusalem? Or at least a synagogue building?

What type of church government should we have?

What should we look for in church leaders?

Do we even need leaders?

What is the purpose of the Lord's Supper?

How often should we eat it? Annually, like Passover?

How should we eat the Lord's Supper (what form should it take)?"

How do you suppose the apostles, the Twelve, would have answered their letter? Would they have written that each church was free to do what ever it wanted to do? That each church should just pray and follow the Holy Spirit's leading? That each congregation should be unique and different, free from outside influence? That the church should be like a chameleon, changing depending on its cultual backdrop? Or, might the apostles have answered with very specific instructions? With a particular way of doing things? With a definite agenda? With unmistakable guidelines?

A problem, faced by believers over the past 2,000 years, concerns exactly what should be done with apostolic patterns for church practice. Should we follow these NT patterns? Is the practice of the early church merely optional or is it imperative for us? Are the traditions of the apostles interesting history or should they constitute some kind of normative church practice?

Our problem is compounded because the NT has almost nothing to say by way of direct command concerning church matters. Currently, it is popular to dismiss NT patterns as optional. Fee and Stuart, two Bible professors in Massachusetts, in *How To Read The Bible For All Its Worth*, state: "Our assumption, along with many others, is that unless Scripture explicitly tells us we must do something, what is merely narrated or described can never function in a normative way" (p. 97, first edition). No one, for instance, would advocate following Jephthah's example in Jdg 11:29ff. The question for us is whether or not Scripture "explicitly tells us" that we "must" copy the patterns for church described in the NT.

Suppose we "bought into" the notion that NT patterns are not to be normative. Into what might this lead us?

1. First, we could construct a massive, opulent cathedral and post on its walls our motto, "Nothing But Positive Command Shall Bind Us" (that should really pack the pews!).
2. We could meet on Tuesdays rather than on Sunday, the Lord's Day (this way we will have less competition from the mainline churches; we will be the un-church).
3. Next, we will meet monthly, rather than weekly (this will be more to the liking of the modern generation, which dislikes commitment).
4. We might also opt to have no leaders at all (no pastors, no elders, no deacons) since no where in Scripture are we directly commanded to have any. This will be popular in America, the land of rugged individualism.
5. We could have absolutely no form of church government whatsoever; ours will be rule by anarchy (every man can just do what is right in his own eyes in fulfillment of Jdg 21:25). No particular form of government is commanded.
6. The Lord's Supper can be celebrated every ten years or so (we wouldn't want it to become too common and lose its significance).
7. Since the NT does not specifically prohibit it, we can swell our membership ranks by baptizing infants or the deceased (1Co 15:29).
8. Finally, new believers could be organized into loose confederations of Bible studies, not official churches (the NT never states we must form churches).

Obviously, this hypothetical "church" would be quite absurd. Yet, technically it would violate no positive command of Scripture. What would be missing is at least a partial adherence to NT patterns for church practice. Most churches do follow some of the patterns of the NT, but not all. The question is, *why not?* That which is argued for in this study is a little consistency. We propose that the apostles had a definite, very particular way they organized churches, AND that they intended for all churches to follow these same apostolic patterns, even today.

### HOLDING TO APOSTOLIC TRADITION IS LOGICAL

1Co 4:14-17 reveals that Paul planned to send Timothy to Corinth. He wanted Timothy to remind the Corinthians of Paul's way of life so that they could imitate Paul. Thus he wrote, "I urge you to imitate me. For this reason I am sending to you Timothy, my son whom I love, who is faithful in the Lord. He will remind you of my way of life in Christ Jesus, which agrees with what I teach everywhere in every church."

Notice the uniformity of practice that is implied in 1Co 4:17b. Paul's way of life in Christ was consistent with ("agrees with") what Paul taught "everywhere in every church". There was integrity. It is an engineering axiom that form follows function. Paul's way of life (form) was in agreement with what he taught (function) everywhere in every church. There was a uniformity of practice that grew out of Paul's teachings. His belief determined his behavior. His doctrine determined his duty. Similarly, the apostles' beliefs about the function of the church would naturally have affected the way they organized churches (the form of the church). Thus, holding to apostolic tradition is logical.

If anyone understood the purpose of the church, the apostles did. They were hand picked and hand trained by Jesus over a three year period. Then, our Lord spent forty days with them after His resurrection. Finally, He sent the Holy Spirit to uniquely teach them things Jesus never did (Jn 14-16). Thus, whatever Jesus taught His apostles about the church was reflected in the way they set up and organized churches.

In Tit 1:5 Paul wrote to Titus, "the reason I left you in Crete was that you might straighten out what was left unfinished . . . " It is evident from Tit 1:5 that the apostles did indeed have a definite way they wanted things done. It was not left up to each individual church to find its own way of doing things. There was obviously some kind of order, pattern, or tradition, that was followed in organizing the churches. Thus, In 1Co 11:34, Paul wrote, "the rest I will set in order when I come" (KJV).

The first Southern Baptist theologian who ever really wrote anything was J. L. Dagg. A founding member of First Baptist Church of Atlanta and professor of theology at Mercer University in Macon, Georgia, Dagg wrote in 1858 that the apostles "have taught us by example how to organize and govern churches. We have no right to reject their instruction and captiously insist that nothing but positive command shall bind us. Instead of choosing to walk in a way of our own devising, we should take pleasure to walk in the footsteps of those holy men from whom we have received the word of life . . . respect for the Spirit by which they were led should induce us to prefer their modes of organization and government to such as our inferior wisdom might suggest" (*Manual of Church Order,* p. 84-86).

### HOLDING TO APOSTOLIC TRADITION IS PRAISEWORTHY

In 1Co 10:31-11:1 Paul urged the Corinthians to "follow" his example: "So whatever you eat or drink or whatever you do, do it all for the glory of God. Do not cause anyone to stumble, whether Jews, Greeks or the church of God - even as I try to please everybody in every way. For I am not seeking my own good, but the good of many, so that they may be saved."

The immediate context concerned seeking the good of others, pleasing others, so as to be used by God in bringing them to salvation. The word "follow" (1Co 11:1) is from *mimatai,* basis for our word "mimic." This command for them to mimic Paul about not being a stumbling block evidently brought to mind a new situation the Corinthians were experiencing, one in which they did a good job of mimicking him: head coverings. Thus he began in 11:2 with, "I praise you because you remember me in everything, and hold firmly to the traditions, just as I delivered them to you" (NASV).

The regular Greek word for "teaching" is *didaskalia* (basis for "didactic"), but that is not the word used here. Instead, *paradosis* ("tradition") is used. Thus, the NASV has "traditions" here rather than "teachings" (NIV). A tradition is "that which is handed down" (information, custom), according to BAGD, p. 615. Webster says it is an inherited pattern of thought or action. A street definition would be, "things people *do* on a regular basis." This same Greek word (in verb from) is used in 1Co 11:23 ("passed on") in regard to the Lord's Supper. The point of a tradition is that it is something that is passed on, from generation to generation.

Next, consider the word, "everything" (1Co 11:2). The word "everything" means "all that exists" or at least "all that pertains to the subject" (Webster). When Paul wrote "everything" (1Co 11:2), what did he have in mind? How might "everything" apply to church order? Use of the word "everything" suggests that Paul's intended application is larger than just the exhortation found in 1Co 10:31-11:1 (evangelism). He is now about to move on to that new topic: head coverings.

What do the words "just as" (11:2) indicate about the degree of their compliance with Paul's "traditions"? They adhered to every iota; it was sort of a photocopy effect! Paul praised them for holding to his traditions "just as" (*kathos*) he passed them on to them. The apostles evidently designed for the churches to mimic the traditions (inherited patterns) they established. The particular issue dealt with in 1Co 11 is the issue of head coverings.

An interesting paradox can be observed about tradition. The same word (*paradosis*) used by Paul in 1Co 11:2 was also used by Jesus in Mt 15:1-3. Jesus said to the Pharisees, "why do you break the command of God for the sake of your tradition?" Amazingly, whereas Jesus blasted the tradition of the Pharisees, Paul blessed the Corinthians for following the tradition of an apostle. Jewish tradition broke the command of God. Apostolic tradition is consistent with the commands of Jesus. Holding to the tradition of the apostles is thus praise worthy, as seen in Paul's praise for the Corinthians.

## HOLDING TO APOSTOLIC TRADITION IS TO BE UNIVERSAL

It is interesting to note how Paul quieted those inclined to be contentious about Christian order. To do so, he made an appeal to the universal practice of all the other churches: "If anyone wants to be contentious about this, we have no other practice - nor do the churches of God" (1Co 11:16).

This statement was supposed to impress the contentious people, to carry weight, to settle the argument. Obviously prior emphasis had been given to certain practices that were done the same way everywhere, and that were supposed to be done the same way everywhere. Thus, 1Co 11:16 further indicates a uniformity of "practice" in NT churches.

It is beyond the scope of this study to deal with the particulars of head coverings. The point is that Paul expected all churches to be doing the same thing. Just to realize that one was "different" was argument enough to silence opposition.

In 1Co 14:33b-34, something else was said to be true in "all" congregations (plural): "As in all the congregations of the saints, women should remain silent in the churches." Regardless of the correct application of this verse, notice how Paul again appeals to a universal pattern in all the churches as a basis for conformity. Thus, 1Co 14:33b-34 indicates a uniformity of practice in NT churches.

Next, notice how Paul chided the Corinthians in 1Co 14:36, "Did the word of God originate with you? Or are you the only people it has reached?" The obvious answer to both questions is "no." Paul's chide in 1Co 14:36 further indicates a uniformity of practice among NT churches. The chide came for doing something different from what all the other churches were doing. Evidently all the churches were expected to follow the same patterns in their church meetings. Holding to apostolic tradition is to be universal.

Jim Elliot, missionary martyr, wrote, "The pivot point hangs on whether or not God has revealed a universal pattern for the church in the New Testament. If He has not, then anything will do so long as it works. But I am convinced that nothing so dear to the heart of Christ as His Bride should be left without explicit instructions as to her corporate conduct. I am further convinced that the 20th century has in no way simulated this pattern in its method of 'churching' a community . . . it is incumbent upon me, if God has a pattern for the church, to find and establish that pattern, at all costs" (*Shadow of The Almighty: Life and Testimony of Jim Elliot*).

## HOLDING TO APOSTOLIC TRADITION BRINGS GOD'S PEACEFUL PRESENCE

The main point of Php 4:4-7 is that we are to rejoice in the Lord, to have God's peace, regardless of circumstances: "Rejoice in the Lord always, I will say it again: Rejoice! Let your gentleness be evident to all. The Lord is near. Do not be anxious about anything, but in everything, by prayer and petition, with thanksgiving, present your requests to God. And the peace of God, which transcends all understanding, will guard your hearts and your minds in Christ Jesus."

"Good bye" is a shortened form of "God Be With You." In the next paragraph of his letter (Php 4:8-9), the church at Philippi is given the secret for how to have the God of Peace be with them. By extension, this can be true for our churches as well: "Finally, brothers, whatever is true, whatever is noble, whatever is right, whatever is pure, whatever is lovely, whatever is admirable - if anything is excellent or praiseworthy - think about such things. Whatever you have learned or received or heard from me, or seen in me - put into practice. And the God of peace will be with you."

Php 4:8 is a popular memory verse, for obvious reasons. Yet the more 4:8 is emphasized, the more 4:9 seems neglected. In 4:9, the Philippians were instructed to put into practice "whatever" they

16

learned, received, heard from Paul, or saw in Paul. Would this "whatever" not also include the way we see in the NT that Paul organized churches? To neglect apostolic tradition is to bypass God's blessing!

Watchman Nee, in *The Church And The Work: Rethinking The Work*, wrote, "Acts is the 'genesis' of the church's history, and the Church in the time of Paul is the 'genesis' of the Spirit's work . . . we must return to 'the beginning.' Only what God has set forth as our example in the beginning is the eternal Will of God. It is the Divine standard and our pattern for all time . . . God has revealed His Will, not only by giving orders, but by having certain things done in His church, so that in the ages to come others might simply look at the pattern and know His will" (p. 8-9).

### HOLDING TO APOSTOLIC TRADITION IS COMMANDED

In 2Th 2:15, the Thessalonian church was instructed to "stand firm and hold to the traditions which you were taught, whether by word of mouth or by letter from us." "Traditions" is from the same word, *paradosis*, used back in 1Co 11:2. The Thessalonians were specifically commanded to follow, to hold to, the traditions of the apostles, whether received by mouth or by letter (whether oral or written). The apostles are not here to tell us in person, by word of "mouth", what to do. However, we do have their "written" directions. The overall context of 2Th 2 refers to a correct understanding of end-time events. But would it not also apply to church order?

Many believers feel that while apostolic tradition is interesting, following it is never commanded. But what does 2Th 2:15 indicate about this issue? Is adherence to the traditions commanded or suggested? Significantly, it is clearly commanded. We are to follow the apostles, not just in their teaching and theology, but also their practice.

A similar attitude is expressed in 2Th 3:6-7a, "keep away from every brother who is idle and does not live according to the traditions you received from us. For you yourselves know how you ought to follow our example." The specific context here refers to gainful work versus being idle and lazy, yet the underlying principle holds true also. The apostles generally wanted the churches to follow, to hold to, their traditions.

Roger Williams, founder of Rhode Island and of the first Baptist church in the Americas (1600s), is another example of a Christian who believed that churches should strive for as near approximate as possible to NT forms and ordinances (*Liberty of Conscience*, p. 106). This belief led Williams to resign the professional pastorate to found Rhode

# Ekklesia . . . To The Roots of Biblical Church Life

Island on the NT pattern of a separation between church and state.

## CONSISTENCE

What can we conclude about God's interest in our own churches adhering to NT patterns for church practice? It seems evident that whatever was normative church practice for all the churches in the NT should be normative practice for churches today. I believe that It was precisely these patterns of church practice that gave the NT church the dynamic that today's church has been missing for so long!

If the Bible directly commands something, then we obviously ought to follow that command. Significantly, the Bible commands adherence to the traditions of the apostles. If, however, the Bible is silent about something (i.e., there is neither command nor pattern to follow), then we have the freedom to do whatever suits us (following the wisdom of the Holy Spirit). The real question thus is not, "Do we have to do things the way they were done in the NT?" The question is: "Why would we want to do things any other way?!"

The Roman world is gone forever. There is a big difference between holding to apostolic tradition versus mindlessly copying everything seen in the NT (wearing sandals, writing on parchment, studying by oil lamps, wearing togas, etc.). The key is to focus in on NT church practice. Of course we must also beware of making patterns out of things that are not patterns in the NT. For instance, the Christian "communism" of Ac 6 was a one time event for a single church. It is an option for any believers of any age, but it is neither a command nor a NT pattern. The same could be said of Paul's vow in Acts not to cut his hair.

What are some apostolic traditions that should still be binding on the church today?
1. The Lord's Supper eaten as a full meal.
2. The Lord's Supper partaken of weekly.
3. The Lord's Supper eaten as the main reason for meeting each week.
4. Interactive, participatory, open church meetings.
5. Mutual edification, encouragement and fellowship as the goals of church meetings.
6. Church government by consensus (elder-led more so than elder-ruled churches).
7. Locally trained leaders.
8. Church eldership that is male, plural, non-hierarchial, homegrown, servant leadership.

18

9. House churches (smaller congregations).
10. Meeting regularly on the Lord's Day (Sunday).
11. The baptism of believers only.
12. The separation of church and state.
13. A regenerate church body.
14. Children present in the church meeting .
15. A community based church (daily fellowship) .
16. Church reproduction & equipping through the ministry of itinerant church workers (apostles, evangelists).

What we argue for here is a little consistency. Most churches already follow some of these patterns, but not all. The question is, why not? This consistency is especially important since the apostles expected for all churches to follow their traditions "just as" they were handed down. Of course, Jesus must be the center of a church or none of this will work anyway. It would blow apart! As He said, "Apart from Me you can do nothing."

Are there ever acceptable exceptions to following NT patterns? London church elder Beresford Job comments, "We must make sure that we don't let biblically permitted deviations from the norm, because of extenuating circumstances, actually become the norm. Let me illustrate this from baptism. Biblical baptism, like apostolic tradition for the way a church functions, is a command from the Lord. And although it's actual mode isn't anywhere commanded we know from the way the early church did it (apostolic tradition again) that it was to be done upon conversion, with no time lapse, and in water. (The immersion bit I take for granted as that's what the actual word baptism means as a transliteration from the Greek *baptizo*.) Now we would be justly concerned at the notion that we are free to make changes to this whether concerning who is to actually be baptized, it's mode, or indeed it's timing; and we are painfully aware it has been massacred in each of these ways by believers for far too long. So our position would be that, in order for it to be based on the teaching of the Word of God, a person should be baptized upon profession of faith in Jesus, as soon as possible, and by full immersion in water. But let us now address the scenario whereby a bedridden quadriplegic comes to the Lord. Baptism, as biblically commanded and exampled in the New Testament for us, is clearly out of the question in such an instance, yet it is quite clear too that to come up with another more appropriate mode of baptism for such a one would not only be okay, it would be positively incumbent upon us. And in such a circumstance one could technically be out of step with the teaching of scripture, yet be fully submitted to it's intention and spirit. But here is the point: none of what I have just said could possibly apply to the conversion of an able bodied person - the normal mode would have to be employed in order for things to be as the Lord wants. And neither could anyone argue for the baptism of someone who hadn't responded to Jesus by faith, because that would attack the very nature of baptism, even though it's external mode was still in accordance with the scripture."

Church renewal advocate Darryl Erkel has pointed out the "danger of making distinctive NT patterns a form of legalism wherein we begin to look down or distance ourselves from our fellow brothers because they don't quite do it the way that we think it should be done. We should always be careful to not give the impression to others that their church is false or that God can't use their church because they're not following Apostolic patterns as closely as we are. That is nothing but sheer pride! On the other hand, we ought to look for opportunities to respectfully and tactfully demonstrate that there is a better way — one which is more conducive to the spiritual growth of God's people — for the function of the New Testament church is best carried out by the New Testament form of the church!"

Remember the earlier quote by Professors Fee and Stuart that what is merely narrated or descirbed can never funtion in a normative way? In the second edition of their book, they changed their statment somewhat. It now reads, *"unless Scripture explicitly tells us we must do something, what is only narrated or described does not function in a normative way — unless it can be demonstrated on other grounds that the author intended it to function in this way"* (p. 106, second edition). We have attempted to demonstrate that the apostles did indeed design for churches to follow the patterns they laid down for church order.

SUMMARY
1. God directs by pattern (tradition) as well as by percept (teaching).
2. The patterns in the NT are to be binding on the church in all ages and places.
3. Apostolic tradition is equal in authority to apostolic teaching.
4. The bare essentials (the irreducible minimum) of a NT church are: a commitment to apostolic tradition, celebration of the Lord's Supper weekly as a full meal, interactive church meetings, church government by consensus (elder led, not elder ruled), and home-based, home-sized churches.
5. Without Christ at the center of things, the patterns become legal-

ism and death, a hollow form, an empty shell. We need the proper wine skin, but more importantly we need the wine. Both have their place. Either one without the other is problematic.

6. Following NT patterns does not mean blindly attempting to recreated Roman culture (like wearing togas, writing on parchment, lighting by oil lamps, etc.). The issue here is church practice. There should be obvious reasons behind the practices being followed.

7. Following NT patterns does not mean every church will be exactly alike (cookie cutter). Certainly there will be similarity in the basics (see summary # 4 above), but there is also freedom within the boundaries of the form.

8. Biblical house churches are not nearly so program and building oriented as many modern churches are. Because of this, some have mistakenly concluded that we are against organization. Faithfulness to our Lord and His Word necessarily results in a biblical house church that follows God's complete pattern for His church. We are not to be institutional, but we are to be organized. Following the traditions laid down by the apostles means that house churches are to have definite leaders, regular and orderly meetings, active church discipline, and weekly Lord's Supper meals.

Many churches today are firmly entrenched in traditions developed after the close of the apostolic era (often traditions date only from the nineteenth century). Although sympathetic with apostolic tradition, the preference is usually given to more recently developed traditions. In such cases, are we not guilty of nullifying the inspired tradition of the apostles for the sake of our own tradition (Mt 15)? Jude 3 states that the faith was "once for all entrusted to the saints." What authorization have we to tamper with it?

—Steve Atkerson

# THE LORD'S SUPPER: FEAST OR FAMINE?

The meal is potluck, or as we like to say, "pot-providence." Everyone brings something to share with everyone else. When the weather is nice, all the food is placed on a long folding table out in the carport. A smaller card table at one end of the long table contains drinks, cups, forks, napkins, etc. A chest full of ice sits on the floor beside the card table. Kids run wildly around having so much fun that they must be collared by parents and forced to eat something. After a prayer of thanksgiving is offered, people line up, talking and laughing, to serve their plates. In the middle of all the food sits a single loaf of bread next to a large plastic jug containing the fruit of the vine. Each believer partakes of the bread and juice while going through the serving line. The smaller kids are encouraged to occupy one of the few places at a table to eat. (They sure can be messy!) Chairs for adults (there are not enough for everyone) are clustered in circles, mainly occupied by the womenfolk, who eat while discussing home schooling, child training, sewing, an upcoming church social, the new church we hope to start, etc. Most of the men stand to eat, balancing their plates on top of their cups, grouped into small clusters and solving the world's problems or pondering some hot topic of theology. The atmosphere is not unlike that of a wedding banquet. It is a great time of fellowship, encouragement, edification, friendship, caring, catching-up, getting to know, praying with, exhorting, and maturing. The reason for the event? In case you did not recognize it, this is the Lord's Supper, New Testament style!

Foreign though it may seem to the contemporary church, the first century church enjoyed the Lord's Supper as a banquet that foreshadowed the marriage supper of the Lamb. It was not until after the close of the New Testament era that the early church fathers altered the Lord's Supper from its pristine form into a memorial service. We advocate a return to the way of Christ and His apostles.

## ITS FORM & FOCUS: A FEAST & THE FUTURE

The very first Lord's Supper is also called the Last Supper, because it was the last meal Jesus shared with his disciples before His crucifixion. The occasion for the meal was the Passover. At this Passover Feast, Jesus and His disciples reclined at a table heaped with food

(Ex 12, De 16). Jewish tradition tells us that this meal typically lasted for hours. During the course of the meal, "while they were eating" (Mt 26:26), Jesus took a loaf bread and compared it to his body. He had already taken up a cup and had them all drink from it. Later, "after the supper" (Lk 22:20), Jesus took the cup again and compared it to his blood, which was soon to be poured out. Thus, the bread and wine of the Lord's Supper were introduced in the context of a full meal (the Passover). Would the Twelve have somehow deduced that the newly instituted Lord's Supper was not to be a true meal? Or would they naturally have assumed it to be a feast, just like the Passover?

"The Passover celebrated two events, the deliverance from Egypt and the anticipated coming Messianic deliverance" (Reinecker, *Linguistic Key to the Greek* NT, p. 207). Soon after that Last Supper, Jesus became the ultimate sacrificial Passover Lamb, suffering on the cross to deliver His people from their sins. Jesus keenly desired to eat that Passover with His disciples, saying that He would "not eat it again until it finds fulfillment in the kingdom of God" (Lk 22:16). Note that Jesus looked forward to a time when He could "eat" the Passover "again" in the kingdom of God. The "fulfillment" (Lk 22:16) of this evidently was later written about by John in Re 19:7-9. There, an angel declared, "Blessed are those who are invited to the wedding supper of the Lamb!" The Last Supper and the early church's Lord's Suppers all looked forward to a fulfillment in the wedding supper of the Lamb. (And what better way to typify a banquet than with a banquet?)

His future wedding banquet was much on our Lord's mind that night. He mentioned it first at the beginning of the Passover feast (Lk 22:16). He mentioned it again when passing the cup, saying, "I will not drink again of the fruit of the vine until the kingdom of God comes" (Lk 22:18). Then, after the supper, He referred to it yet again, saying, "I confer on you a kingdom . . . so that you may eat and drink at my table in my kingdom . . ." (Lk 22:29-30).

Whereas twenty-first century Gentiles associate heaven with clouds and harps, first century Jews thought of heaven as a time of feasting at Messiah's table. This idea of eating and drinking at the Messiah's table was common imagery in Jewish thought of the first century. For instance, a Jewish leader once said to Jesus, "Blessed is the man who will eat at the feast in the kingdom of God" (Lk 14:15). In Mt 8:11 Jesus Himself said that "many will come from the east and the west, and will take their places at the feast with Abraham, Isaac and Jacob in the kingdom of heaven."

The eating that is associated with the coming of Christ's kingdom

## Chapter 2: The Lord's Supper: Feast or Famine?

is even seen in the model prayer of Mt 6:9-11. In reference to the kingdom, Jesus taught us to pray, "your kingdom come, your will be done." The very next sentence is "Give us today our daily bread." Interestingly, the Greek underlying Mt 6:11 is difficult to translate. Literally, it reads something akin to, "the bread of us belonging to the coming day give us today." Linking 6:11 with 6:10, Jesus may well have been teaching us to ask that the bread of the Messianic (kingdom come) banquet be given to us today. I.e., let the kingdom come and the feast begin today!

The most extensive treatment of the Lord's Supper is found in 1 Corinthians 10 - 11. The deep divisions of the Corinthian believers resulted in their Lord's Supper meetings doing more harm than good (11:17-18). They were partaking of the Supper in a "unworthy manner" (11:27). Evidently the rich, not wanting to eat with the lower social classes, came to the meeting so early and remained there so long that some became drunk. Making matters worse, by the time that the working class believers arrived, delayed by employment constraints, all the food was gone and they went home hungry (11:21-22). Some of the Corinthians failed to recognize that the Supper as a sacred, covenant meal (11:23-32). The abuses were so bad that it had ceased being the Lord's Supper and had instead become their "own" supper (11:21, NASV). Thus Paul asked, "Don't you have homes to eat and drink in?" If merely eating ones own supper were the objective, private dining at home would do. Their sinful selfishness absolutely betrayed the very essence of what the Lord's Supper is all about.

From the nature of their abuse of the supper, it is evident that the Corinthian church regularly partook of the Lord's Supper as a true meal. In contrast, no one today would ever come to a typical Lord's Supper service expecting to have physical hunger satisfied, nor could they possibly get drunk from drinking a thimble sized cup of wine (or much less, grape juice). However, the inspired solution to the Corinthian abuse of the Supper was not that the church cease eating it as a full meal. Instead, Paul wrote, "when you come together to eat, wait for each other." Only those so famished or undisciplined or selfish that they could not wait for the others are instructed to "eat at home" (1Co 11:34). Paul wrote to the Corinthian church some twenty years after Jesus first turned His Last Supper into our Lord's Supper. Just as the Last Supper was a true meal, so too the Corinthians understood the Lord's Supper to be a true meal.

Further, the word behind "supper" (1Co 11:20) is *deipnon*, which means "dinner, the main meal toward evening, banquet." It never refers to anything less than a true meal, such as an appetizer, snack or *hors d'oeuvres*. How likely is it that the authors of the NT would use *deipnon* to refer to the Lord's "Supper" if it were not supposed to be a true meal? The Lord's Supper originally had numerous forward looking aspects to it. As a full meal, it prefigured the feast of the coming kingdom, the marriage supper of the Lamb.

The opinion of scholars is clearly weighted toward the conclusion that the Lord's Supper was originally eaten as a full meal. Donald Guthrie, in *The Lion Handbook of the Bible*, states that "in the early days the Lord's Supper took place in the course of a communal meal. All brought what food they could and it was shared together." Dr John Drane, in *The New Lion Encyclopedia*, commented that "Jesus instituted this common meal at Passover time, at the last supper shared with His disciples before His death . . . the Lord's Supper looks back to the death of Jesus, and it looks forward to the time when He will come back again. Throughout the New Testament period the Lord's Supper was an actual meal shared in the homes of Christians. It was only much later that the Lord's Supper was moved to a special building and Christian prayers and praises that had developed from the synagogue services and other sources were added to create a grand ceremony." J. G. Simpson, in an entry about the Eucharist in *The Dictionary of the Bible*, observed that "the name Lord's Supper, though legitimately derived from 1 Corinthians 11:20, is not there applied to the sacrament itself, but to the Love Feast or Agape, a meal commemorating the Last Supper, and not yet separated from the Eucharist when St. Paul wrote." Canon Leon Morris, in his *Commentary on 1 Corinthians* for the *Tyndale New Testament Commentaries* insists that 1Co 11 "reveals that at Corinth the Holy Communion was not simply a token meal as with us, but an actual meal. Moreover it seems clear that it was a meal to which each of the participants brought food." I Howard Marshall, in *Christian Beliefs* noted that the Lord's Supper "was observed by His disciples, at first as part of a communal meal, Sunday by Sunday."

### ITS FUNCTIONS: A. REMINDING JESUS

Partaking of the bread and cup as an integral part of the meal originally served several important functions. One of these was to remind Jesus of His promise to return. "Reminding" God of His covenant promises is a thoroughly Scriptural concept. In the covenant God made with Noah, He promised never to destroy the earth by flood again, signified by the rainbow. That sign is certainly designed to remind us of God's promise, but God also declared, "whenever the rainbow appears in the clouds, I will see it and remember the everlasting covenant between God and all living creatures of every kind on the earth" (Ge 9:16 ). Later on in redemptive history, as a part of His covenant with Abraham, God promised to bring the Israelites out of their coming Egyptian bondage. Accordingly, at the appointed time, "God heard their groaning and he remembered his covenant with Abraham, with Isaac and with jacob. So God looked on the Israelites and was concerned about them" (Ex 2:24-25). And during the Babylonian captivity, Ezekiel, records that God promised Jerusalem that He would "remember the covenant I made with you" (Ez 16:60).

The Lord's Supper is the sign of the new covenant. As Jesus took the cup He said, "this is my blood of the covenant, which is poured out for many for the forgiveness of sins" (Mt 26:28). As with any sign, it is to serve as a reminder. Thus Jesus said that we are to partake of the bread "in remembrance of me" (Lk 22:19). The Greek for "remembrance" is *anamnesis* and means "reminder." Literally translated, Jesus said, "do this unto my reminder." The issue before us is whether that reminder is to be primarily for Jesus' benefit or for ours. The prepositional phrase "of me" (or "my") is translated from the single Greek word, *emos*, which grammatically denotes possession (i.e., the reminder belongs to Jesus). Thus, the church was to partake of the bread of the Lord's Supper specifically to remind Jesus of His promise to return and eat the Supper again, in person (Lk 22:16, 18). Understood in this light, it was originally designed to be like a prayer asking Jesus to return ("Thy kingdom come", Mt 6:11). Just as the rainbow reminds God of His covenant with Noah, just like the groaning reminded God of His covenant with Abraham, so too partaking of the bread of the Lord's Supper was designed to remind Jesus of His promise to return. Colin Brown quotes J. Jeremias as understanding Jesus to use *anamnesis* in the sense of a reminder for God, "The Lord's Supper would thus be an enacted prayer" (*NIDNTT*, III, p. 244).

Paul, in 1Co 11:26 confirms this idea by stating that the early church, in eating the Lord's Supper, did actually "proclaim the Lord's death until He comes." To whom did they proclaim His death, and why? Arguably, they proclaimed it to the Lord Himself, as a reminder for Him to return. It is significant that the Greek behind "until" is *achri hou*. When used with the subjuctive, it grammatically can denote a goal, or an objective (Reinecker, *Linguistic Key To The Greek NT*, p. 34). According to the English usage, I may use an umbrella "until" it stops raining, merely denoting a time frame. (Using the umbrella has nothing to do with making it stop raining.) However, this is not how the Greek behind "until' is used in 1Co 11:26. Paul instructed the church to partake of the bread and cup as a means of proclaiming the Lord's death (as a reminder) "until" (so that, with the goal of) persuading Him to come! Thus, in proclaiming His death through the loaf and cup, the Supper looked forward to and anticipated His return.

This idea of seeking to persuade the Lord to return is not unlike the plea of the martyred saints of Re 6 who called out, "How long, Sovereign Lord, holy and true, until you judge the inhabitants of the earth and avenge our blood?" (Re 6:10). And what did Peter have in mind when he wrote that his readers should look forward to the day of God and "speed its coming?" (2Pe 3:12). If it was futile to seek to persuade Jesus to return, then why did Jesus instruct his disciples to pray, "Thy kingdom come, Thy will be done?" (Mt 6:10).

### ITS FUNCTIONS: B. CREATING UNITY

All this emphasis on the Supper as a true meal is not to say that we should jettison the loaf and cup, representative of the body and blood of our Lord. To the contrary, they remain a vital part of the Supper (1Co 11:23-26). But just as the form of the Lord's Supper is important (a full fellowship meal that prefigured the wedding banquet of the Lamb), so too the form of the bread and cup are important. Paul made mention of "the" cup of thanksgiving and of the "one loaf" (1Co 10:16-17). The significance of using but one cup and one loaf in the Supper is "because there is one loaf, we who are many, are one body, for we all partake of the one loaf" (1Co 10:16-17). The one loaf not only pictures our unity in Christ, but according to 1Co 10:17 even creates unity. Notice careful the wording of the inspired text. "Because" there is one loaf, therefore we are one body, "for" we all partake of the one loaf (1Co 10:17). Partaking of a pile of broken cracker crumbs and multiple cups of the fruit of the wine is a picture of disunity, division, and individuality. At the very least, it completely misses the imagery of unity. At worse, it would prohibit the Lord from using the one loaf to create unity in a body of believers.

### ITS FUNCTIONS: C. FELLOWSHIP

In speaking to the church at Laodicea, our resurrected Lord offered to come in and "eat" (*deipneo*) with anyone who hears His voice and opens the door, a picture of fellowship and communion (Re 3:30). The idea that fellowship and acceptance is epitomized by eating together was derived not only from the Hebrew culture of Jesus' day, but also from the earliest Hebrew Scriptures. Ex 18:12 reveals that Jethro,

Moses, Aaron, and all the elders of Israel came to "eat bread" in the "presence of God." More divine dining occurred at the cutting of the Sinai covenant, when Moses, Aaron, Nadab, Abihu and the seventy elders of Israel when up on Mt Sinai where they "saw God, and they ate and drank" (Ex 24:9-11). It is significant that "God did not raise his hand against these leaders" (Ex 24:11a). They were accepted by Him, as evidenced in the holy meal they ate in His presence.

This fellowship in feasting theme is continued on in the book of Acts, where we learn that the early church devoted themselves to "fellowship in the breaking of bread" (2:42, literal translation). In your English version, notice that in Ac 2:42 there is an "and" between "teaching" and "fellowship," and between "bread" and "prayer," but not between "fellowship" and "bread." In the Greek, the words "fellowship" and "breaking of bread" are linked together as simultaneous activities. They had fellowship with one another as they broke bread together. Luke further informs us that this eating was done with "glad and sincere hearts" (2:26). Sounds inviting, doesn't it? Many commentaries associate the phrase, "breaking of bread" throughout the books of Acts with the Lord's Supper. This is because Luke, who wrote Acts, recorded in his gospel that Jesus took bread and "broke it" at the last supper (22:19). If this conclusion is accurate, then early church enjoyed the Lord's Supper as a time of fellowship and gladness, just like one would enjoy at a wedding party.

ITS FREQUENCY: WEEKLY

We have thus seen the original form (a full fellowship meal with one cup and one loaf) and focus (forward looking) of the Lord's Supper. One final and important aspect needs to be considered: its frequency. How often did the New Testament church partake of the Supper? The Roman Catholics have it right on this point. Early believers ate the Lord's Supper weekly, and it was the main purpose for their coming together each Lord's Day.

The first evidence for this is grammatical. The technical term, "Lord's Day" is from a unique phrase in the Greek, *kuriakon hemeran*, which literally reads, "the day belonging to the Lord." The words "belonging to the Lord" are from *kuriakos*, which occurs in the NT only in Re 1:10 and in 1Co 11:20, where Paul uses it to refer to the "Lord's Supper" or the "Supper belonging to the Lord" (*kuriakon deipnon*). The connection between these two uses must not be missed! If the purpose of the weekly church meeting is to observe the Lord's Supper, it only makes sense that this *supper* belonging to the Lord would be eaten on the *day* belonging to the Lord (the first day of the week). John's revelation (Re 1:10) evidently thus occurred on the first day of the week, the day in which Jesus rose from the dead and the day on which the early church met to eat the Supper belonging to the Lord. The resurrection and the day and the supper all go together as a package deal!

Second, the only reason ever given in the New Testament as to the regular purpose for a church meeting is to eat the Lord's Supper. In Ac 20:7, Luke informs us that, "On the first day of the week we came together to break bread." The word "to" in Ac 20:7 is known as a telic infinitive. It denotes a purpose or objective. Their meeting was a meating! Another place in the NT that the purpose for a church gathering is stated is found in 1Co 11:17-22. The "meetings" (11:17) were doing more harm than good because when they came "together as a church" (11:18a) they had divisions so deep that "when you come together, it is not the Lord's Supper you eat" (11:18b). From this is it obvious that the primary reason for their church meetings was to eat the Lord's Supper. Sadly, their abuses of the Supper were so gross that it had ceased being the Lord's Supper, but officially they were gathering each week to celebrate the Supper. The third and last location of a reference to the reason for an assembly is found in 1Co 11:33, "when you come together to eat, wait for each other." As before, it shows that the reason they came together was to "eat." Lest this appear to be making a mountain out of a mole hill, it must be realized that no other reason is ever given in the Scriptures as to the purpose of a regular, weekly church meeting.

The fellowship and encouragement that each member enjoys in such a gathering is tremendous. It is the Christian equivalent of the neighborhood bar. It is the true happy meal or happy hour. It is a time that God uses to create unity in a body of believers. This aspect of the church's meeting should not be rushed or replaced. Certainly it is appropriate to also have a 1Co 14 phase of the gathering (an interactive time of teaching, worship, singing, testimony, prayers, etc.), but not at the expense of the weekly Lord's Supper.

## PRACTICAL CONSIDERATIONS

Practicing the Lord's Supper as a full meal today is can be a means of great blessing to the church. Here are some practical considerations concerning the "how to"s of implementing it.

**Attitude:** Be sure the church understands that the Lord's Supper is the main purpose for the weekly gathering. It is neither optional nor secondary to some type of "worship service". Even if a church only has the Lord's Supper one week, it has fulfilled its primary reason for having a meeting that week.

**Food:** If at all possible, make the meal potluck and purpose to eat whatever it brought. This makes the administration of the food much easier. Trust God's sovereignty! In ten years of doing this, our church only had one Sunday where everyone brought desserts, and even then we solved the "problem" by simply ordering out for pizza! Over-planning the meal can take a lot of the fun out and make it burdensome. The one thing that is pre-planned is who supplies the one loaf and the fruit of the vine. The family that is hosting the meeting always supplies the bread and cup for our church.

**Giving:** Since celebrating the meal is a New Testament pattern and something important to the life of a properly functioning church, money spent by individual families on food to bring is a legitimate giving expense. Rather than merely dropping an offering in a plate each week, go to the grocery store and buy the best food you can afford. Bring it to the Supper as a sacrificial offering!

**Clean Up:** To facilitate clean up, you may want to consider using paper plates and napkins. At our church we do use plastic forks and cups, which need to be washed, but that is because folks sometimes carelessly throw away their utensils along with the rest of their trash. Better to throw away a plastic fork than a metal one! To help avoid spills, the host family supplies wicker plate holders each week, which can be reused and don't usually need to be washed.

**Logistics:** In warm weather it may be appropriate to eat outside, in the shade of a carport or backyard. Spilled food and drink is inevitable, and clean up is much easier outside. A large folding table can be placed where necessary and stored away after the meeting. In cold weather, when eating indoors is necessary, consider covering any nicely upholstered furniture with a layer of plastic and then cloth. Since children make the most mess, reserve any available seating at a table for them and insist they use it!

**The Cup and Loaf:**  Some have found that taking the cup and loaf prior to the meal separates it from the meal too much as a separate act. It is as if the Lord's Supper is the cup and loaf, and everything else is just lunch. To overcome this false dichotomy, try placing the cup and loaf on the table with the rest of the food of the Lord's Supper. The cup and loaf can be pointed out in advance of the meeting and mentioned in the prayer prior to the meal, but then placed on the buffet table with everything else. This way, folks can partake of it as they pass through the serving line. This is a freedom issue.

Should the loaf be unleavened and the fruit of the vine alcoholic? The Jews ate unleavened bread in the Passover meal to symbolize the quickness with which God brought them out of Egypt. Certainly Jesus used unleavened bread in the original Last Supper. However, nothing is said in the NT about Gentile churches using unleavened bread in the Lord's Supper. Though sometimes in the NT yeast is associated with evil (1Co 5:6-8), it is also used to represent God's kingdom (Mt 13:33)! As we see it, it is a matter of freedom. As related to wine, it is clear from 1Co 11 that wine was used in the Lord's Supper (some became drunk). However, no clear theological reason is ever given in Scripture for so doing (but consider Ge 27:28, Isa 25:6-9, Ro 14:21). As with the unleavened bread, it is a freedom issue.

**Unbelievers:** Should unbelievers be allowed to partake of the Lord's Supper? The Lord's Supper, as a sacred, covenant meal, has significance only to believers. To nonbelievers, it is merely food for the belly! It is clear from 1Co 14:23-25 that unbelievers will occasionally attend church meetings. Unbelievers get hungry just like believers do, so invite them to eat too. Love them to Jesus! The danger in taking the Lord's Supper in an unworthy manner applies only to believers (1Co 11:27-32).

Regarding the one cup and loaf, if an unbelieving child desires to drink the grape juice just because he likes grape juice, that is fine. However, if the parents purposely give it to an unbelieving child as a religious act, then that would be a violation of what the Lord's Supper is all about. It would be closely akin to the error of infant baptism.

**Ordained Clergy:** Some traditional churches feel that only an ordained clergyman can officiate at the Lord's table. This is evidently a holdover from Roman Catholicism. The New Testament makes no so such requirements.

CONCLUSION

Now that the New Testament form of the Supper has been duly established, the next question facing believers today concerns our Lord's intent for post-first century churches. Does Jesus desire for His people to celebrate the Lord's Supper in the same way it was eaten in the New Testament? Or could it be a matter of indifference to Him? Do we have the freedom to deviate from the Supper's original form as a true banquet? Why would anyone want to depart from the way Christ and His apostles practiced the Lord's Supper? The apostles plainly were pleased when churches held to their traditions (1Co 11:2) and even commanded that they do so (2Th 2:15). We have no authorization to deviate from it.

To summarize all that has been posited, the Lord's Supper is the primary purpose for which the church is to gather each Lord's Day. Eaten as a full meal, the Supper typifies the wedding supper of the Lamb and is thus forward-looking. It is to be partaken of as a feast, in a joyful, wedding atmosphere rather than in a somber, funeral atmosphere. A major benefit of the Supper as a banquet is the fellowship and encouragement each member experiences. Within the context of this full meal, there is to be one cup and one loaf from which all partake. These are symbolic of Jesus' body and blood and serve to remind Jesus of His promise to return. The one loaf is to be used not only to symbolize the unity of a body of believers but also because God will use it to create unity within a body of believers.

— Steve Atkerson

# 3
## *INTERACTIVE MEETINGS*

The first song begins promptly at 10:30 a.m. Prior to that, folks are milling about talking, hauling in food or kids, getting a cup of coffee from the kitchen, hugging and greeting each other, etc. That first song is the cue for everyone to assemble in the living room so that the more formal time of the informal meeting can begin. There are usually about ten families and two singles present. Counting kids, that is around fifty people. Some are usually late in arriving. There are typically enough chairs for the adults, and the kids sit on the floor near their parents. Young children color or play quietly with toys during the entire meeting. The dress code is casual, comfortable, and informal.

The musicians (two tenor banjos, one guitar and a mandolin) do not try to be worship leaders. Their goal is simply to facilitate and support the group's singing. As many or as few songs are sung as are requested. Spontaneous prayer is often offered between songs, sometimes leading to longer times of conversational prayer. There is no bulletin or order of service, though everything is done in a fitting and orderly way. One person at a time may speak. The "prime directive" is that anything said or done must be designed to build up, edify, encourage or strengthen the whole church.

Sometimes several brothers teach. Some weeks no one brings a word of instruction. Certainly those burdened to instruct prepare prior to the meeting, but rarely is anyone officially slated to do so. Interspersed between the songs and teachings, testimonies are shared of God's provision, lessons learned, prayers answered, encouraging events, etc. Not infrequently a visiting Christian worker will report on his ministry and God's movings in other places.

It is not a show or performance. There is neither moderator nor emcee. Unless there is a problem to resolve, a visitor would not even know who the leaders are. Sometimes there are a periods of silence. There is not an official ending time for the meeting. Often it lasts one and a half to two hours. Either everyone who desires to sing or speak has done so, or the kids are at the end of their endurance, or hunger motivates a conclusion. It is generally ended with prayer. Afterwards, folks stay and fellowship as long as they desire. Often, the meeting transitions into the Lord's Supper (depending on which came first that week, the meeting or the meating!).

The church meeting described above is not fictional. Such meetings take place every Lord's Day, all over the world. They even occur in such unlikely places as England, America, Canada, Australia and New Zealand! They are modeled after the church meetings described in the New Testament. Western believers are often so accustomed to holding church in special sanctuaries with stained glass, steeples, pipe organs, pews, pulpits, choirs bulletins, and worship leaders that it is assumed Scripture dictates such trappings. The reality is that New Testament church meetings were vastly different from what typically goes on today.

### SCRIPTURAL ARGUMENTS FOR INTERACTIVE MEETINGS

The crux of the matter lies with a question Paul asked the Corinthians, "What then shall we say, brothers? When you come together, everyone has a hymn, or a word of instruction, a revelation, a tongue, or an interpretation. All of these must be done for the strengthening of the church" (1Co 14:26). Had Scripture used the words "only one" instead of "everyone," the verse would be more descriptive of a modern worship service. However, it is clear from the text that those original church meetings were anything but a spectator's sport. There was interaction, spontaneity, and participation. In a sense there was no audience because each of the brothers was potentially a cast member.

The spontaneous and interactive nature of their meetings is also evident in the regulations concerning those who spoke in tongues: "If anyone speaks in a tongue, two - or at the most three, should speak, one a time, and someone must interpret. If there is no interpreter, the speaker should keep quiet in the church and speak to himself and God" (1Co 14: 27-28). Were these speakers in unknown tongues scheduled in advance to speak? Not likely, given the supernatural nature of the gift. That the meetings were interactive is evident from the fact that up to three people could speak in tongues and in the need for an interpreter to be present.

Further indication of the participatory nature of their gatherings is seen in the guidelines given for prophets (1Co 14:29-32). First, we are informed that "two or three prophets should speak, and the others should weigh carefully what is said" (14:29). The spontaneous nature of their participation comes out in 14:30-31a, "if a revelation comes to someone who is sitting down, the first speaker should stop. For you can all prophesy in turn . . . " Clearly, some of the prophets came to church on "empty", not planning to say anything, but received a revelation while sitting there listening.

One of the most controversial paragraphs in the New Testament occurs in 1Co 14:33b-35, regarding the silence of women in the meeting. Whatever it was that the women were not supposed to say, there would have been no need to write that unless first century church meetings were participatory. It is obvious from 14:35 that people were asking questions of the speakers during the church meetings: "If they want to inquire about something, they should ask their own husbands at home . . .". Even if Paul only meant that women were not to be the ones doing the questioning, it still remained that the men were free to quiz a speaker. The point to be gleaned is that a church meeting is not supposed to be a one way communication. There is to be dialog, interaction, a give and take exchange between the speaker and the church.

Almost every New Testament letter is an "occasional document," so-called because it was written in response to some local problem. Evidently some in Corinth wanted to conduct their meetings differently than this passage requires. Clearly, some aspect of the church meetings in Corinth was amiss. This much is obvious from the nature of the two questions asked of them: "Did the word of God originate with you? Or are you the only people it has reached?" (1Co 14:36). The word of God had, in fact, not originated with the Corinthians, and they most certainly were not the only people it had reached. These questions were thus designed to convince them that they had no right nor authorization to conduct their meetings in any other way than that prescribed in 1Co 14. The inspired correction was for the church to have regulated, orderly interaction, and not a prohibition of it: "be eager to prophesy, and do not forbid speaking in tongues. But everything should be done in a fitting and orderly way" (14:39-40). In fact, holding church meetings in this spontaneous, interactive manner is declared to be imperative in 1Co14:37, "If anybody thinks he is a prophet or spiritually gifted, let him acknowledge that what I am writing to you is the Lord's command.". Thus, 1Co 14 is not merely descriptive of primitive church meetings, it actually is prescriptive of the way our Lord wants meetings of the whole church conducted.

It is really not surprising that the meetings of the early church would have been interactive. The first believers in most areas of the Roman Empire had Jewish backgrounds. They were accustomed to typical synagogue format, which was open to participation from those in attendance. An examination of Ac 13:14-15, 14:1, 17:1-2, 17:10, 18:4 and 19:8 will reveal that the apostles could never have evangelized the way they did unless the synagogues allowed audience input. The apostles were always allowed to speak in the open meetings of the synagogue. In fact, if those first century synagogue meetings were anything like our typical twenty-first century Western church worship services, Paul and his companions would have had to find another way to reach the Jews with the gospel.

There are other indicators as well. In Ac 20:7, we discover that Paul "kept on talking" ("preached," KJV) to the church at Troas until midnight. The Greek behind "talking" is *dialegomia* which actually means "consider and discuss, argue." Our English word "dialogue" is derived from it today. Further, the author of Hebrews urged his readers to "not give up meeting together, as some are in the habit of doing, but let us encourage one another" (10:25). The "one another" aspect of his instruction most naturally fits into such an interactive setting.

The over-arching goal given in 1Co 14 for anything said or sung in a church meeting is the "strengthening of the church" (14:26). The Greek word used here is *oikodome*, "building up" (BAGD, p. 559) or "edification" (NASV). Thayer pointed out in his lexicon that it is the action of one who promotes another's growth in Christianity. Thus, any remark made in a church meeting has to be designed to help the church. It must be calculated to encourage, build up, strengthen, or edify the other believers present. Paul encouraged prophecy over a public address in tongues because everyone who prophesied in a church meeting spoke to men for their "strengthening, encouragement and comfort" (1Co 14:3) with the result that the church was "edified" (14:5). The Corinthians were instructed to "try to excel in gifts that build up the church" (14:12). This emphasis on edification is also seen in Heb 10:24-25 where believers are told to meet together in order to stimulate each other to love and good deeds and to "encourage" one another.

One final observation needs to be made concerning those pristine church meetings: their purpose. In today's gatherings, congregations are inspired to worship by impressive architecture, massive choirs, thundering pipe organs, and thrilling orations. Such a meeting is commonly called a "worship service." This title suggests that the primary reason for the gathering is to worship God. Yet oddly, the New Testament never refers to a church meeting as a "worship service." Paul, in Ro 12:1-2, did make mention of a "spiritual service of worship" (NASV), but this referred to a life of holiness, not an assembly of saints.

Many things can contribute to the strengthening of the church, including corporate worship. Worship, however, is not the only activity that can edify. The problem lies partially in naming the meeting a "worship service." First, church meetings are to be interactive, not a "service." Second, such a title suggests that worship is the only appropriate activity that is to occur. Other modes of edification are seen as out of order. People are led to expect emotional feelings such as are associated with cathedral architecture, candles, hushed sanctuaries, stained glass, awe-inspiring music, and the presentation of a program that is in essence a performance. With such unbiblical expectations, a truly biblical 1Co 14 meeting will seem strange, uncomfortable, or disconcerting.

Jesus told the woman at the well that "a time is coming when you will worship the Father neither on this mountain nor in Jerusalem," (Jn 4:21-24). He so saying, he made it clear that the new covenant worship has nothing to do with any particular location or time. It transcends 11:00 a.m. Sunday morning and should not be localized in any church "sanctuary." There are primarily two Greek words in the NT for "worship." The first is *proskuneo* and refers to an attitude of adoring awe toward God. It is humility toward the Father. It is reverence, appreciation, fear, and wonder. This attitude of inner devotion is very practically worked out in the second word for worship (*latreia*), which refers to a life-style of obedience and service. Worship is thus *both* an attitude and an action. As Francis Scott Key penned in a hymn: "And since words can never measure, let my life show forth Thy praise." Thus, while our participation in the weekly church meeting is undeniably an act of worship, so is going to work everyday, spanking our children, loving our families, etc. Under the new covenant, all of life is holy.

The Sunday gathering is for the benefit of the people present. It is not God who needs strengthening because He is not weak. The Lord doesn't need to be encouraged since He is neither tired nor discouraged. Jesus is not lacking in anything, but His people certainly are. The purpose of a church meeting is to equip God's people to go out to worship and serve God another week (Heb 10:24-25). It is to motivate the elect to deeper worship and obedience. It is to recharge their spiritual batteries.

### LOGICAL ARGUMENTS FOR INTERACTIVE MEETINGS

It is fact of history that the early church met in the homes of its members. No special church buildings were constructed during the New Testament era, nor or for the following two hundred years. This necessarily meant that their meetings were smaller rather than larger. This smaller setting argues against the possibility that those pristine meetings consisted of an eloquent sermon delivered to a massed crowd of hushed listeners.

After Christianity was made the official religion of the Roman

Empire, pagan temples were turned by government decree into church buildings. Believers were herded out of their home meetings and into large basilicas. Such huge gatherings are not conducive to participatory meetings, so naturally they became more of a show or "service." Any interactive teaching necessarily turned into a monologue presentation, preaching or oration. Questions from the "audience" were not allowed. Spontaneity was lost. The "one another" aspect of an assembly became impossible. Informality gave way to formality. Church leaders began to wear special costumes. Worship aids were introduced: incense, icons, hand gestures, etc. Today, even the songs are picked in advance by gifted musicians. In short, the New Testament way was jettisoned for a way of man's own devising.

The issue is which type of church meeting best meets the needs of God's people? Certainly much good comes from the weekly proclamation of God's Word by those church leaders who have come to be known as "preachers." Also beneficial is the worshipful and inspirational singing of the great hymns of the Faith. Yet there is supposed to be more to a church meeting than merely "attending" a "service." To allow any of the brothers who so desire to verbally participate in the meeting also allows for a greater working of the Spirit as various ministry gifts begin to function. Not allowing them to function causes atrophy and even apathy. God may burden several brothers, independent of each other, to bring a teaching. Learning is increased as questions are asked of a speaker. Additional applications and illustrations can be offered to a word of instruction by the body at large. False doctrines can be judged and exposed publicly, at the point of presentation. New believers learn how to think biblically and with the mind of Christ as more mature believers are seen reasoning together and interacting with each other. Maturity rates skyrocket. The brothers begin to "own" the meeting, taking responsibility for what goes on, and become actively involved.

### SCHOLARLY TESTIMONY FOR INTERACTIVE MEETINGS

That New Testament church gatherings were completely open and participatory with no one leading from the front is agreed upon by researchers. For instance, Dr. Henry R Sefton, in *A Lion Handbook - The History of Christianity*, stated, "Worship in the house-church had been of an intimate kind in which all present had taken an active part . . . (this) changed from being 'a corporate action of the whole church' into 'a service said by the clergy to which the laity listened'" (p. 51).

Dr. John Drane, in *Introducing the New Testament,* wrote that "In the earliest days . . . their worship was spontaneous. This seems to have been regarded as the ideal, for when Paul describes how a church meeting should proceed he depicts a Spirit-led participation by many, if not all . . . There was the fact that anyone had the freedom to participate in such worship. In the ideal situation, when everyone was inspired by the Holy Spirit, this was the perfect expression of Christian freedom" (p. 42).

A. M. Renwick, writing in *The Story of the Church*, said that "The very essence of church organization and Christian life and worship . . . was simplicity . . . Their worship was free and spontaneous under the guidance of the Holy Spirit, and had not yet become inflexible through the use of manuals of devotion" (p. 22-23).

PRACTICAL CONSIDERATIONS

One aspect of New Testament meetings that is still familiar today is the singing. The Ephesian church was instructed to "speak to one another with psalms, hymns, and spiritual songs. Sing and make music in your heart of the Lord" (Ep 5:19). Similarly, the Colossians were exhorted to "let the word of Christ dwell in your richly as you teach and admonish one another with all wisdom, and as you sing psalms, hymns, and spiritual songs with gratitude in your hearts to God" (Col 3:16). Perhaps not so familiar to modern believers is the "one another" (Ep 5:19, Col 3:16) aspect of the music. According to 1Co 14:26, "everyone" of the brothers had the opportunity to bring a "hymn." No mention is made anywhere in the New Testament of a minister of music or worship leader dominating, leading or controlling the singing. It is a blessing to have gifted musicians in a congregation who can assist the church in worship and singing. However, to be true to the New Testament prescription, that person must be careful not to carry on a running monologue nor perform like a singer on a stage. The brothers of the church must be given the freedom and responsibility of requesting whatever songs are sung, and whenever they are sung.

On a related note (pun intended), some folks are adamantly against the use of musical instruments in church meetings. The Greek word for "hymn" (1Co 14:26) translates *psalmos*, which fundamentally means, "songs accompanied by a stringed instrument". Since instruments are not forbidden, and since there is no pattern of specifically not using them, we feel that this is a freedom issue.

Another feature of early church meetings that continues today is the teaching of God's Word. Our Lord instructed the apostles to baptize all nations, "teaching them to obey everything I have commanded you"

(Mt 28:20). Accordingly, we learn from Ac 2:42 that the Jerusalem church "devoted themselves to the apostles' teaching." Further, "teaching" is listed as a spiritual gift in Ro 12:7 and 1Co 12:28. And, one of the requirements of an elder is that he be "able to teach" (1Ti 3:2). Elders who work hard at "teaching" (1Ti 5:17-18) are worthy of "double honor" (financial support). However, in 1Co 14, teaching is tossed in with the other activities in an almost cavalier way. The teacher is not given the prominence that one sees in today's typical church meeting. "Everyone" of the "brothers" was to be given the opportunity to contribute a "word of instruction" (14:26). What this demands for us today is first an appreciation of the importance of a teaching ministry, yet allowing for any brother who so desires to be given the opportunity to teach. Practically, it would also suggest each teaching be shorter rather than a longer in order to allow "air time" for others who might desire to teach.

Amazingly, pastors are not even mentioned in 1Co 14. This may be because pastors did not dominate these types of gatherings with their teachings. This is not to say that elders did not teach in the meetings, but it is clear from 1Co 14 that non-elders also had the opportunity to do so. Thus the author of Hebrews made the general statement that "by this time you ought to be teachers" (Heb 5:12). That he did not have the leaders in mind is evident from his salutation ("greet all your leaders," 13:24), revealing that he did not even expect the elders to read the letter! Still though, just because the opportunity exists for someone to teach, it does not necessarily follow that they should teach. The elders must remind the church of the warning that "not many of you should presume to be teachers, my brothers, because you know that we who teach will be judged more strictly" (Jam 3:1). James' warning makes sense in light of the intimate, interactive meetings that characterized the early church.

This freedom for any brother to teach is precisely when the elders are needed most. If a brother brings an erroneous teaching or application, it is up to the elders to point the error out. Timothy, an apostolic worker stationed temporarily at Ephesus, was to "command certain men not to teach false doctrines any longer" (1Ti 1:3). One qualification for an elder is that he must "hold firmly to the trustworthy message as it has been taught, so that he can encourage others by sound doctrine and refute those who oppose it" (Tit 1:9). Titus was told to "encourage and rebuke with all authority. Do not let anyone despise you" (Tit 2:15). Thus the aged apostle John warned about a known deceiver: "do not take him into your house." This would be especially applicable to house churches with participatory meetings.

No one would argue with the truth that some brothers are far more qualified to teach than are others. An aged, godly man, gifted to teach, who loves the Lord, and who has studied the Bible and served people all his life, is going to have profound insights to share with the church. In the presence of such men the rest of us should be "quick the listen, slow to speak" (Jam 1:19). Special times should be devoted to allow such a man the opportunity of expounding God's Word. However, such meetings are what Watchman Nee called "worker's meetings" or "apostolic meetings", not 1Co 14 church meetings. The point is that there is a time and a place for both.

Charismatic churches are quite familiar with revelations, tongues, and interpretations. Churches that practice such gifts should be sure the guidelines of 1Co 14:26-32 are followed closely. Un-interpreted tongues are not to be allowed. There is to be a cap on the number of those who do speak in tongues. Only one person at a time should speak. Prophecies must be judged, and anyone who desires to prophesy needs to realize in advance that his words will be weighed carefully. Doubtless much that passes for prophecy and tongues is bogus. Dealing with them can be messy and frustrating since overly emotional and unhinged folks often imagine they have such gifts. Perhaps that is why the Thessalonians had to be told, "do not treat prophecies with contempt. Test everything. Hold on to the good. Avoid every kind of evil" (1Th 4:20-22). And, in the midst of all these supernatural utterances, there must be order: "The spirits of the prophets are subject to the control of the prophets. God is not a God of disorder but of peace" (1Co 14:32). Elders play a key role in help everything that goes on in the meeting to be done in a "fitting and orderly way" (1Co 14:40).

Other churches believe that charismatic gifts ended in the first century, or have no one present so gifted. Even so, the principle of participatory meetings remains. Brothers should still be free to spontaneously bring teachings, request or introduce songs, share testimonies, offer prayer, question speakers, etc. Yet despite our theological suspicions, it should give pause to read Scripture clearly instruct, "do not forbid to speak in tongues" (14:39). Perhaps tongues have indeed ceased, but maybe not. Are we really so sure of our theology that we are willing to directly contradict a biblical command?

Another practical consideration for participatory meetings concerns the idea of a moderator or emcee. Notice that none is mentioned in 1Co 14. As a church matures in experiencing interactive gatherings, the need for someone to moderate the meeting will diminish. Ideally, a visitor to a properly functioning church would not even know who its leaders were unless there was a problem that required correction.

A "warning shot across the bow" was fired by the inspired writer in 1Co 14:38. After stating that these orderly, interactive meetings are the "Lord's command" (14:37), he then cautioned that anyone who disregards what was written would be "ignored." Though unclear as to exactly what this meant, some type of penalty was threatened. A price will be paid for disregarding the "Lord's command" for church meetings.

The authors of this book have many combined years of practical experience with participatory meetings. We have observed that there are some typical problems to be expected. We detail these below in the hope that being forewarned is being forearmed!

**Pew Potatoes.** Most church folks, after years of attending services, are conditioned to sit silently, as if watching TV. It takes time and prompting to over come this. Participating meaningfully will seem awkward to people at first. Continual prompting and encouraging during the week may be necessary until people "break the sound barrier." Is there a testimony the Lord would have you to bring? Is there a song that would edify the church? Is there some subject or passage of Scripture to teach on? If a string were stretched across a stream at water level, various things would become attached to it as the day passed, things that otherwise would have floated on past. Similarly, thinking all week long about what to bring to the meeting helps greatly. If no one brought food for the agape love feast, there would not be much of a feast. Similarly, if no one comes to the meeting prepared to contribute, there will not be much of a meeting! Men, do your wives spend more time preparing for church (by cooking food for the Agape feast) that you do (in considering something to say in the meeting)?

**Unedifying Remarks.** Sometimes after folks do start talking, they get a little too casual. Chitchat abounds. Just because it is an "open" meeting does not mean people can say anything they want to say. Leaders need to remind the church that anything said in the meeting must be designed to build up the body, to encourage everyone else. As Peter said, "If anyone speaks, he should do it as speaking the very words of God" (1Pe 4:11). Church meetings are also not to be therapy sessions for the wounded, with everything focused on one person and his needs. Though such people do need counseling, it is generally to be done at a time other than the corporate assembly (the same as in 1Co 14:4).

**Pooled Ignorance.** This is the opposite of bringing a teaching. It is sort of an anti-teaching. Rather than study a subject in advance to bring a teaching, some folks will come to the meeting totally unprepared and simply plop a question out before the gathered church for an answer. Discourage people from asking such questions to the church out of ignorance. It only edifies the person asking the question and is not designed to edify the church. It is too "me" oriented. It is asked to meet a personal need. Since no one else will have recently studied the topic anyhow, the temptation will be to answer the question and pooled ignorance will likely abound. There simply is no substitute for the careful, systematic, in-depth study of Scripture in private and in advance of the meeting, and no excuse for not so doing.

**Over-Scheduled Meetings.** Those used to church bulletins will want to arrange teaching, music, etc. in advance. Beware of quenching the Spirit! It is clear from 1Co 14 that New Testament church meetings were generally spontaneous.

**Disruptive Visitors.** Uninformed guests can easily hijack a meeting by unedifying remarks. Egomaniacs will try to take over. The mentally unstable will speak loudly and often, to the chagrin of the assembly. Critics may attack what the church does or believes in the meeting. Leaders are needed in such cases to restore order with wisdom and patience. Visitors must be prompted in advance of the divine guidelines found in 1Co 14. An ounce of prevention is worth a pound of cure! (See the sample prospective visitor's letter at the end). It may be appropriate to invite the critic to air his opinions later, after the meeting is over, during the fellowship of the Lord's Supper or in a midweek study called for that purpose.

**Population Control.** Meetings that are either too big or too small create their own set of hindrances to interactive gatherings. Too few people can seem dull. Too many people present will intimidate the shy and work against open sharing.

**Worship Leaders.** Musicians are to facilitate the church's singing and worship, not control it. Beware of worship leaders who would take over the meeting and make it into a show.

**Punctuality.** Relation-based churches are notoriously bad about starting late. If it is announced that a meeting will begin at a certain time, then the leaders need to be sure that it does start at that time. It is a matter of courtesy and respect for the value of other people's time. Arriving on time also shows respect. Consistently being late for a meeting is often a sign of passive aggression. At the very least it is rude and inconsiderate.

**The emcee.** Some leaders will tend to want to emcee the meetings, as if they were television talk-show hosts. Perhaps such prompting will be necessary in the infancy of a church, but in maturity this will not be needed. Further, there is nothing wrong with silence occasionally. Trust the Holy Spirit to guide the assembly. Ideally, a visitor in a 1Co 14 meeting should not be able to tell who the elders are in the church. Unless there is a problem, the elders should just blend into the woodwork! Admittedly, lack of participation on the part of the body can be a problem, so elders may need to lead out more in such cases to encourage input from others.

**Children.** The NT pattern seems to be for children to be present in the meeting with their parents. Paul intended some of his letters to be read aloud to the entire church (Col 4:16). Based on Ep 6:1-3, children were present in NT church meetings, not shunted off some place else, or they would not have been there to hear Paul's instructions to them when the letter was read. Cp also Mt 19:13-15, Lk 2:41-50, Ac 21:5. However, very small children who begin crying loudly in the meeting need to be removed from the meeting by a parent until the child is quieted. Older children must be taught to sit still or play silently on the floor so as not to disrupt the meeting. Some parents will be oblivious to this need and in such cases the leadership must speak to the parents in private to enlist their cooperation in controlling their children.

**False expectations.** People will invariably come to the 1Co 14 with preconceived notions of what the meeting should be like. For instance, some will want a moving worship service, or to sing only the great hymns of the faith, or will exclusively associate praise songs with heartfelt worship, or expect dramatic healings to take place, or a high powered bible lecture, or emotional presentations of the gospel. Failure to realize these expectations will result in disappointment and discontentment. Church leaders need to be aware of this and take steps to help people have biblical expectations of the meetings, to have the same goals that our Lord does.

#### OBJECTIONS

Some overseers voice vigorous objection to this type of church meeting. With good reason they fear that chaos and anarchy could break out. It must be remembered however that while there is order in a cemetery, there is no life there. It is better have life and risk a little disorder! Keeping order is one of the duties of an elder. Church leaders are also responsible for training the saints so that they are equipped to contribute meaningfully to such a meeting and to judge error for themselves. Further, the Holy Spirit must be trusted to work in the life of a church. If the Scriptures truly reveal God's desire for participatory meetings, then God will also see to it that the meetings will be successful in the long run.

Frankly, some pastors will oppose the guidelines of 1Co14 precisely because enacting them will result in a lack of focus on the pastor. Sadly, a small percentage of pastors are on ego trips or have their need for self affirmation fulfilled by being the "star player" in a service. This is a blind-spot that must be overcome and repented of.

Impedance to the commands of 1Co 14 can also occur if believers become so intoxicated with their newly found freedom that they essentially run off into anarchy or gnosticism. They become overly wary of "agendas." To them, anyone with leadership inclinations or skills is somehow self-willed or evil. Yet it is obvious that Paul had a "agenda" for the churches he ministered to. Balance is a key consideration. We need to be about the Lord's agenda of helping His churches come into compliance with everything the Lord commanded!

Not a few people have read 1Co 14 and judged their churches to be in utter compliance because the congregation participates through responsive readings, genuflecting, partaking of the wafer and wine of the Lord's Supper, singing hymns, giving tithes and offerings, etc. Part of the problem is that all of this is planned out, the structure is the same every week, and the entire order of worship is laid out in the bulletin. There may be limited audience participation, but there is no real liberty. Is any one of the brothers free to pick a hymn? To bring a teaching? To raise his hand and ask a question? Is their spontaneity?

### CONCLUSION: AFFIRMATIONS & DENIALS

What conclusions can be drawn about the way God desires the weekly, Lord's Day church meeting to be conducted? We affirm that:

1. The meeting is to be participatory and spontaneous.
2. Anything said or done must be designed to strengthen (edify) the whole church.
3. Only one person at a time is to address the assembly.
4. Everything is to be done in a fitting and orderly way
5. One of an elder's roles in such meetings to keep it "on track" and true to the prime directive that all things be done unto edifying. 5.
6. This type of interactive meeting is not optional, is not just interesting history, is not just quaint information. Such meetings are the "Lord's command" (1Co 14:37).

We deny that:

1. "Worship services" were held by the New Testament church.
2. Huge assemblies of Christians meeting for weekly worship is a NT pattern.
3. Church meetings need to be led from the front by a worship leader.
4. Bulletins are necessary or even slightly beneficial to a church meeting.
5. Only one person can teach in the meeting.
6. Teachers should be scheduled in advance.
7. Ritual and ceremony were part of NT church meetings.
8. Special aids to worship are important, such as incense, special costumes, icons, statues, stained glass, or ornate cathedral-like buildings.
9. Performance-like shows are legitimate substitutes for the NT prescription.

— Steve Atkerson

A LETTER TO PROSPECTIVE VISITORS

"We are honored that you have expressed an interest in visiting one of our church meetings. We have made a conscious effort to seek to follow the traditions of the original apostles in our church practice. Thus, even though we are in one sense quite "traditional", what we do is rather non-conventional by contemporary standards. Anyhow, the following will give you a good idea of what to expect. Our hope is that you will feel comfortable and encouraged when meeting with us.

Our original church has grown into two churches. Though interdependent, each is ultimately autonomous. One meets in the morning and the other in the evening, both in NE Oz, just off the Yellow Brick Road. For location and directions, please call:

**Morning Church**:
John & Violet Calvin  770-493-1234
Charles and Daisy Spurgeon  770-938-1234
**Evening Church**
Jonathan & Marigold Edwards  770-908-1234
George and Rose Whitfield  770-455-1234

Following the pattern of the NT, each church comes together regularly on the first day of each week. This is known in Scripture as the Lord's Day, the day Jesus conquered death and rose from the grave. We do not, however, see it as any type of sabbath day. Every day is a holy day under the New Covenant (Heb 4, Col 2:16 - 17, Ga 4:8-11).

The doors of the host's home open at either 10 a.m. (for our morning church) or 4 p.m. (for our evening church) and the singing starts promptly one half hour later. Thus you can see that there is a 30 minute window for folks to come in, get settled, visit, get coffee, etc. Please try to park on the same side of the street on which the home is located. This will make it less likely that our cars will choke up the neighborhood street.

Our dress code is casual and comfortable. Nobody wears a tie. Ladies wear anything from comfortable dresses to pants to modest shorts. Children usually end up playing outside after the meeting and therefore wear play clothes and shoes. Getting dirty is not uncommon for the kids.

The meeting itself is spontaneous and interactive (no bulletin!) per 1Co 14:25ff. Nothing is pre-planned except the starting time of the first song (10:30 a.m. or 4:30 p.m.). Sometimes we sing a lot, sometimes not much at all. On one Sunday three brothers may teach, while on

49

other weeks no one will teach. Sometimes we pray a long time, sometimes very little. All the brothers can participate verbally, but everything said must be designed to edify the whole church (14:26). Only one person at a time is allowed to address the assembly, and everything is to be done in a fitting and orderly way. All teaching and prophecies are liable to public cross examination and judgment. Further, there is no moderator nor emcee per se. In fact, unless there is a problem to correct, you will not even know who our leaders are (we have two elders)!

Inquiring minds will want to know that most of us hold to the doctrines of grace, new covenant theology (www.ids.org), biblical inerrancy, and the Danvers statement on biblical manhood and womanhood (www.cbmw.org). You can find out more about biblical house churches at www.ntrf.org.

The children stay with us in the meeting, though if a really young child gets noisy one of his parents will take him out until he calms down. If you have young children you may wish to bring along something to keep them happy, such as a drawing pad and crayons or quiet toys. The kids usually sit on the floor next to their parents. We believe it is the parent's job to teach their children about Jesus, not the church's. Thus, we purposely have no Sunday school nor children's church.

Ladies do not speak out or pray publicly in the 1Co 14 meeting (yes, we know this is hard to believe, but look up 1Co 14:33-35 and you'll see where this comes from). In contrast, the sisters do speak quite a bit during the fellowship of the Lord's Supper!

The Lord's Supper is an integral part of our gathering and starts around noon. Actually, it is the main reason we come together each week. We eat it as a full meal per 1Co 11b. It is potluck with everyone bringing something to share with the rest. We believe it is to be a true meal to typify the wedding banquet of the Lamb. It's a great time of fellowship and encouragement and very much like a wedding party rather than a funeral. In the middle of all the food you will notice the one cup (plastic jug, actually) and the one loaf, representing the body and blood of our Lord. We believe it was originally designed to remind Jesus of His promise to return and partake of the meal again with His people. Feel free to partake of the bread and the fruit of the vine as you go through the food line. There is not an official ending time. Just leave after you have dined and enjoyed sufficient fellowship!

In short, we believe that the patterns for church life evident in the New Testament are not merely descriptive, but are actually prescriptive (2Th 2:15, 1Co 11:2). Thus, we believe in home-based and sized fellowships, elder led rather than elder ruled churches, the ministry of itin-erant workers, interactive meetings, and that the Lord's Supper and the Agape Feast are synonymous weekly events. You may find it helpful to read through 1Co 11:17-34 and 1Co 14:26-40 before coming.

For us, true church "life" occurs every day, as we see each other during the week, all week long. To facilitate this, we place a high prior-ity on living as close together as is practice. The core group all lives in the same neighborhood. So, the Lord's Day activities described above are just the icing on the cake. To evaluate us based solely on what you observe in a Sunday meeting would be an incomplete analysis!

Our churches are committed to meeting and living out as simple as possible a reading and understanding of what the NT church gave us for a pattern. We know we don't have it all figured out yet. We are a work in progress! We tend to take issues one at a time and attempt to come to a biblically based consensus before moving on. Everybody counts and ideally nobody gets run over or discounted. This means we sometimes move pretty slow, but with a high degree of peace and unity. For that we have been blessed and are grateful.

See you on the Lord's Day!"

THE NEW TESTAMENT WAY OF MEETING

How is it then, brethren?  When ye come together, everyone of you hath a psalm, hath a doctrine, hath a tongue, hath a
revelation, hath an interpretation.  Let all things be done unto
edifying.

If any man speak in an unknown tongue, let it be by two or
at the most by three, and that by course, and let one interpret.
But if there be no interpreter, let him keep silence in the church;
and let him speak to himself, and to God.

Let the prophets speak two or three, and let the other judge.
If anything be revealed to another that sitteth by, let the first
hold his peace.  For ye may all prophesy one by one, that all
may learn, and all may be comforted.  And the spirits of the
prophets are subject to the prophets.  For God is not the author
of confusion, but of peace, as in all the churches of the saints.

Let your women keep silence in the churches: for it is not
permitted unto them to speak; but they are commanded to be
under obedience, as also saith the law.  And if they will learn
anything, let them ask their husbands at home: for it is a shame
for a woman to speak in the church.  What! Came the word of
God out from you? Or came it to you only?

If any man think himself to be a prophet, or spiritual, let
him acknowledge that the things that I write unto you are the
commandments of the Lord.  But if any man be ignorant, let him
be ignorant.

Wherefore, brethren, covet to prophesy, and forbid not to
speak with tongues.  Let all things be done decently, and in
order.

— 1Co 14:26-40 (KJV)

## OUR MODERN WAY OF MEETING

How is it then, brethren? When ye come together, the pastor hath a doctrine, and the minister of music hath psalms. Let all things be done unto worship.

If anyone besides the pastor hath a doctrine, let him not speak; let him hold his peace. Let him sit in the pew, and face the back of the neck of the person which sitteth ahead of him.

Let the people keep silence in the churches: for it is not permitted unto them to speak; but they are commanded to be under obedience, as also saith church tradition. But if they will learn anything, let them ask their pastor after the service, for it is a shame for a layman to speak in the church. For the pastor, he hath a seminary degree, and the layman, he hath not so lofty a degree.

If any man desire to remain a church member in good standing, let him acknowledge that what I write to you is the command of the denominational headquarters. But if any man ignore this, he shall be promptly escorted out the door by the ushers.

Wherefore brothers, covet not to speak in the church. Let all things be done decently and in the order in which it hath been written in the church bulletin.

— Rusty Entrekin

"We are a society with a common religious feeling, unity of discipline, a common bond of hope. We meet in gatherings and congregations to approach God in prayer, massing our forces to surround Him . .
. We meet to read the divine Scriptures . . . Our presidents are elders of
proved character . . .

Even if there is a treasury of a sort, it is not made up of money paid
in initiation fees, as if religion were a matter of contract. Every man
once a month brings some modest contribution – or whenever he wishes,
and only if he does wish, and if he can; for nobody is compelled; it is a
voluntary offering . . . to feed the poor and to bury them, for boys and
girls who lack property and parents, and then for slaves grown old . . .

So we, who are united in mind and soul, have no hesitation about
sharing property. All is common among us – except our wives. At that
point we dissolve our
partnership . . .

Our dinner shows its idea in its name; it is called by the Greek
name for love . . . We do not take our places at table until we have first
partaken of prayer to God. Only so much is eaten as satisfies hunger.
After water for the hands come the lights; and then each, from what he
knows of the Holy Scriptures, or from his own heart, is called before the
rest to sing to God.

Prayer in like manner ends the banquet . . ."

(*Roman Civilization Source Book II: The Empire*, p. 588)

*Tertullian  lived around 200 A.D.*

*4*

# PREACHING & TEACHING

**PART ONE**

For 1900 years the Christian Church has been largely based on teachings and practices from sources other than the Word of God, and this has left us with a real legacy of things that desperately need to be corrected as far as church practice is concerned. Part of that legacy is that we have departed quite drastically from the way Bible teaching and corporate instruction was done in the early church, and by far the most serious departure in this regard is the virtually universal practice of revolving the gathering of the church on the Lord's Day around preaching and teaching, as done by one person.

In the New Testament, however, we see something rather different. What we find there is churches meeting on Sundays, in people's houses, and with a twofold purpose. Firstly, they had completely open, participatory and spontaneous sharing together and worship which, by definition, wasn't led from the front in any way. Secondly, they ate the Lord's Supper together as their main meal of the day. Given such a set up, and it is indeed how the apostles universally set churches up to be like, then certain things would subsequently, and quite logically, find no place.

For instance, in such a set up there is not the slightest need for religious or sacred buildings, and so it will come as no surprise that we therefore find the churches in the New Testament meeting exclusively in people's homes. And something else you won't find in the New Testament either is a Sunday service, led from the front, with those attending sitting audience style in rows and participating only in singing and, maybe, a bit of open prayer and the like. Neither will you find in the New Testament anything that even faintly resembles a sermon. And of course the reason is that such a practice would go completely against what the very essence of a church gathering on Sundays was seen to be. The apostles set churches up in such a way that when they came together on the Lord's Day the rule was strictly, "each one has . . . for you may all prophesy one by one" (1Co 14:26, 31). They set churches up in such a way that would positively encourage all those gathered to participate, and therefore brought about a situation where the Lord would be free to move by His Spirit through each part of His body. Any idea of the

Lord's Day gathering of the church revolving around the ministry of any one individual flies completely in the face of scripture and contradicts it outright.

This is not to say, however, that there isn't a place for the type of teaching amongst God's people whereby one person predominates in giving it. The Lord does indeed provide people in churches who are gifted in this very thing, and the New Testament makes it clear that teaching is a calling and gift of the Holy Spirit. Indeed, in the church of which I am a part we meet for Bible study on Tuesday evenings, and we work very hard at furthering our understanding of God's Word. But in the New Testament the coming together of a church on Sundays was not the time when such gifts were exercised in that particular way, and the push was always for mutual participation; for lots of people to share something, including a short teaching, rather than for one person to predominate or lead in any way.

And this helps us to at last take the emphasis away from leadership, and from our wretched inclination to just revolve around those who are gifted in teaching and public speaking ability and make big men of them. It helps to keep us safe from the evil of the whole clergy/laity divide and from the completely unbiblical two-tier system of the leaders and the led which creates hierarchy. Hierarchy is something no church should ever have, and the only hierarchy found in the pages of the New Testament pertaining to church life is simply Jesus and everyone else. Even elders - for that is what a biblically based church will either have or be moving towards, a plurality of co-equal, male elders who have been raised up from among those they serve - are strictly in the "everyone else" category.

Moreover, this biblical way of doing things we are seeing creates a set up in which people feel free to question whatever is being taught in order to test and understand it more fully. It also makes those who teach realise that the onus is on them to do so in such a way as to persuade people that what they are saying is actually biblical. It helps minimise the danger of those who are taught being expected to just passively accept things because it's what the leaders teach, or because of some daft idea of "accepted church policy" or something. It brings about a situation wherein people are much more likely to actively and questioningly understand rather than merely passively accept things as being the case and just agree. It creates, in short, what many leaders in many churches fear most, people with open Bibles and free-thinking minds who don't accept things merely on the authority of a leader's say-so, but who question and challenge until they are persuaded that something is or isn't biblical. It further releases the corporate insight and wisdom of all in the church, and engenders an atmosphere of humble attitudes and the willingness for everyone to learn from anyone. It recognises the vitally important fact that the Lord is in all His people and can therefore speak through any of those in the church and not just some chosen and verbally gifted elite.

But I must deal now with what might, in some people's minds, be perceived as a real and biblically based objection to what I'm writing here. So let's turn to the Acts of the Apostles and take a look at a particular Sunday that Paul the Apostle spent with the church in Troas: "On the first day of the week we came together to break bread. Paul spoke to the people and, because he intended to leave the next day, kept on talking until midnight" (Ac 20:7).

Here we have the believers in Troas coming together for their main weekly gathering, and we can note certain things (By the way, no Bible scholar would disagree with any of the following observations I am going to make. They are a simple matter of textual fact): that the church gathered on the first day of the week, on Sunday, that they were gathered together in someone's housethat the Greek text here conveys that the main purpose given for their gathering was to break bread, and that the phrase "breaking of bread" refers to eating a full meal, probably the Lord's Supper.

Now the thing I want to home in on here is that that Paul, "spoke to the people" and "kept on talking until midnight." That certainly makes it sound as if Paul is doing the talking and that everyone else is just listening. So if that is the case then there isn't much open, un-led participatory stuff going on here as we might expect to see, assuming of course that what I've written so far isn't complete nonsense. But there's worse to come, because in some translations of the Bible this verse reads like this, "Paul preached unto them...and continued his speech until midnight."

That doesn't just sound like a Sunday sermon, it sounds like the very mother and father of all Sunday sermons either before or since! Paul, if this verse is to believed, not only preached to the church, but continued to do so until midnight. What on earth can I say to that in the light of the burden of this article? Well, it's actually very simple, because what we have here is an example of bad translation. The original Greek doesn't say here quite what the translators would have you believe, and Luke doesn't use any of the various Greek words for "preach" at all, but rather describes what Paul was doing here until midnight with the word *dialogemai*. And *dialogemai*, as any Greek scholar will tell, means to converse, to discuss, to reason or dispute with. It denotes a two-way discussion between different parties and is actually the Greek word from which we get the English word dialogue.

Preaching is a monologue, and in certain settings of church life that may well be fine. Mid-week Bible studies, for example, may also be done by one person doing a monologue followed by questions. But in the New Testament, when the Lord's people come together on Sundays as a church, it's strictly dialogue that goes on, and this is precisely what Paul is doing here. He is most certainly teaching the church, and it goes on most of the night because they wanted to learn all they could from him, but it was a discussion-type format, not a monologue of some kind. It was participatory and interactive, and therefore completely in keeping with the way Sunday gatherings of a church were set up to be like. In short, Paul was simply conversing with them. It was a dialogue, and he and the assembled church were reasoning together. It was two-way, mutual communication, question and answer, point and counter-point, objection and explanation! Paul isn't here standing on some raised platform with everyone sitting silently just listening to him speaking at them; he is rather sitting on the sofa in the lounge talking with them. There is indeed a time, as I have already said, for something of a more formal lecture type format, but even then let it be clear that whoever is teaching must be completely and fully open to questions concerning their subject matter. I don't by that necessarily mean in the middle of the teaching. Let whoever is doing it finish first, of course, but afterwards let the questions and comeback readily flow. And let it be clear too that whoever does do teaching is just one of the brothers, and not someone special or spiritually elevated just because they are gifted in a particular way. And even on our Tuesday night Bible Studies at the church I am part of we do lots of discussion and interactive type teaching sessions as well, and use the lecture type format as just one of various approaches.

Let me end by making clear that we are here far from downplaying Bible teaching in the life of Christian churches. Far from it! Indeed, none of us would be going on about any of these things in the first place were it not for the fact we are into good solid Bible teaching ourselves, and keen to both receive it and to pass it on to others. No, we are simply saying that we have got to start doing things right and biblically, and that we must in this, as with everything else, get back in line with what the Word of God teaches, rather than just sticking with age-old, yet completely unbiblical, traditions.

Churches need ongoing teaching, of that there can be no doubt, but they need other things too; and to do some biblical things at the expense of other equally biblical things is a big mistake. The apostles expected that when believers met in their respective churches on the Lord's Day then it would be a case of, "When you come together each one has" (1Co14:26). That is the way it should be! Nothing more and nothing less!

Got it then? Good! It's pretty simple really, isn't it? After all, whose ideas do you think have got to be the best: Jesus and His apostles, or someone else's?

— Beresford Job

PART TWO

In the past few months several people have asked me questions about the proper place of "Bible study" in the assembly. For those in traditional churches fulfilling the above verse translates into being faithful to come and hear a "sermon" every Sunday morning in a church building. Those who have felt led to pursue *ekklesia* in more informal settings usually have questions about how "teaching" fits into the new scheme of things. Not a few, in reacting to the previous centrality of the pulpit, are leery of being "taught" by anybody, or fear that one person will dominate. Some feel that body gatherings should focus on *relational* issues instead of studying the Bible. Others feel that there must be teaching every week, or the saints will dry up. What can we learn from the New Testament to put these various concerns in proper perspective?

After 3000 people believed and were baptized, "they devoted themselves to the apostles' teaching and to the fellowship [*koinonia*], to the breaking of bread and to prayer" (Ac 2:42). We see here four central characteristics that marked the believers' life together. The apostles were immediately involved in teaching the flock. So it is clear that *teaching* is very important in the *ekklesia*. But the teaching occurred in the setting of *koinonia*, eating and praying together.

Among the many gifts Christ gives to his people, some are gifted as *teachers* (Ep 4:11). James says, "Not many of you should presume to be teachers, my brothers, because you know that we who teach will be judged more strictly" (3:1). Paul says, "if a person's gift is teaching, let him teach" (Ro12:6-7). And in 1Co12:28-29 Paul underscores the fact that Christ never intended for everybody to have the same gifting by asking, "Are all teachers?" On the other hand, the writer to the Hebrews chides *all the brethren* for their lack of growth by saying, "though by this time you ought to be teachers, you need someone to teach you the elementary truths of God's word all over again" (5:12).

So while it is clear that only *some* are gifted as teachers, all of Christ's people are to be "teachers" in the broad sense of contributing to the overall edification of the body according to their gifting.

Obviously, groups of believers will vary greatly in their giftedness, but if the Lord has brought them together, they can be sure that "in fact God has arranged the parts in the body, every one of them, just as he wanted them to be" (1Co12:18). Some assemblies will have several gifted at teaching, some will have one person, and others may feel that they have none. The central thing to keep in mind is that all believers have the Holy Spirit (the "anointing") and are capable of some level of sharing Christ, of manifesting discernment, of caring for one another, and of understanding the Scriptures. When they come together in His name, they have every reason to expect Christ's presence (Mt18:20). In a *body meeting*, each person present has the responsibility to make sure they do not dominate and thereby stifle others. If there are multiple teachers, none should dominate. If there appears to be only one teacher, care should be taken that that gift should not end up being in the limelight. If there appear to be none gifted as teachers, then the body must work hard at trusting the Lord for edifying multiple participation. We are so used to the artificial thinking that assumes that teachers must have a background in a Bible School or seminary. This is not a Scriptural mindset. We must neither succumb to the cult of the expert, not mute any eminent gifts in the body.

In Ac 20:7 we are specifically told that the purpose of the saints' gathering was to "break bread," not to hear teaching. However, in the course of that particular meeting – which was to be Paul's last appearance in their city — the apostle "dialogued" with them for a long time. What Paul had to say was the meat of the meeting, but it was not a monologue. It was discourse with interaction. This shows that while the *raison d'etre* of the meeting was to eat (the Lord's Supper), it was still possible for teaching to take place.

The Corinthians evidently felt that everybody should speak in tongues. They were focusing on certain visible manifestations of the Spirit. Paul corrects this in 1Co12-14. In chapter 14, he wants the spontaneity and multiple participation to continue, but in all of this he desires for *prophecy to be central*, and for *everything to be done for edification*. Prophecy by "all" results in *strengthening, encouragement, comfort and instruction* (14:3, 31). In verse 26, Paul mentions a few of many possible contributions that the saints can make to the meeting, and one of them is "a teaching." So, just as we should not forbid tongues (if there is interpretation), neither should we forbid teaching!

One thing that would help assemblies in all these issues surrounding "teaching" is if they would *learn how to study the Bible together with a view toward discerning the Lord's mind and acting upon it*. Since there is so much false teaching floating around, it is vital for *ekklesias* to search the Scriptures to see what is actually so. For example, on a host of topics — prayer, angels, body-life, humility, and love — it is certainly possible for a group of believers to photocopy from a concordance or print out from a computer a selection of verses to go over together in discussion and prayer. In the early church *apostolic epistles* were read to the assembly. That is something congregations should do with regularity. It must be stressed that any handling of God's word by an *ekklesia* should not be approached as a *stale, intellectual, academic exercise*. Our goal must be to exalt Jesus Christ together and obey what he reveals in his word.

Congregations will have their strengths and weaknesses. Some will be grounded in sound teaching, but weak in prayer. Some will excel in mutual caring, but be weak in some gospel truths. The general trend I have seen is that churches tend to be *all doctrine with little body-life*, or *focused on subjective experience with little sound teaching*. Why do we sever what God has joined together? We should strive to be *caring, practical fellowships who, as Paul exhorted, wish to hold fast to healthy teaching*. Therefore, brethren should always be evaluating their life together in light of a summary text like Ac 2:42, and openly discuss areas they need to grow in.

James 1:19 exhorts all of us to be "quick to hear and slow to speak." In any group of saints there will be those who tend to talk a lot, those who are reticent, and others inbetween. Those who are always ready to speak must be cautious and be sure they do not stifle the input of others. They must be careful not to dominate or to intimidate by a dogmatic tone that shuts down discussion. Those who are very hesitant to speak need an atmosphere of acceptance and love where they can be encouraged to share as the Lord leads them. If our meetings are truly *open*, then we must be sensitive to the direction of the Spirit's leading. We must each be willing to defer to the needs of others. For example, if a body has new converts, or people who have just come out of a cult, or people who just experienced a major life-altering trauma, it will be necessary to focus on their special needs.

A big issue for all of us is the ability to listen carefully to the concerns of others in the body. If we really love each other, we will want to process the issues on other people's hearts. We may think their question or concern is misplaced, irrelevant, or a non-issue to us, but if

61

we value them we will take their every word seriously.  Thus, if you find yourself internalizing thoughts like, "this place is becoming like an arid seminary," "I can't keep up with the fine theological points that are being made," "all we talk about are people's experiences and we never get into the Word," "we study the Bible a lot but do not pray much," "we go through pretty much the same rut every week," "I'm feeling depressed and not encouraged when I leave the meeting," "So-and-so seems to dominate the meeting every week," "I sense a doctrinal imbalance is taking place," etc., you need to talk with the brothers and sisters.  The problem may be you and your wrong perceptions, but when people have concerns they *must* be openly addressed.  That is why is appears wise for an assembly to periodically discuss how their life together is going, so imbalances can be nipped in the bud.

The chemistry of each assembly is unique.  The Spirit will take the things of Christ and apply them to our circumstances.  What works for one group won't make sense in another group.  But nothing will work unless the brethren are committed to pursuing the Gospel together, in humility preferring one another.  The basic components of church life are given in the New Testament, and the odds are high (given the example of the seven *ekklesias* Christ evaluated) that every assembly has undealt with weaknesses that require change and repentance.  Over the long haul together we need the proper mix of *teaching, singing, eating, praising, praying, caring*, and many other attributes, in order to be healthy.  Most of our concerns about how *teaching* comes to expression in an assembly would probably be resolved if more open discussion with one another and listening to one another were taking place.

— Jon Zens

# 5

# THE PASTOR'S AUTHORITY

Authority seems to be an issue for Christians these days. People write book after book and preach sermon after sermon about who has authority over whom and why. Teachers must teach with authority; husbands claim authority over their wives, "shepherds" need authority over their "sheep." We can't talk about church without concentrating on church government. We seem unable to think about marriage without asking who has authority in it. And we can't even listen to the Bible unless we have first heard the latest word on its authority. Seems to be a problem.

Maybe it is more of a problem in America because we don't usually think of ourselves as subject to authority. We think of ourselves as "free," able to do as we please. Even so, our lives are filled with people and structures which demand our obedience. The police officer on the corner and the IRS have authority. Authority is not just the ability to compel another person. We call that "power." Power is shared by both cops and robbers. Yet only the cop has "authority" – the morally legitimated ability to compel another. Indeed, this is our common notion of authority – it is a legitimated ability to compel another, backed (if need be) by force. Yet this common notion doesn't work when transferred into Christian contexts, for Jesus and his disciples have a very different vision of authority.

Jesus' disturbing teaching about authority among his followers contrasts their experience of it with every other society. The kings of the Gentiles, he said, lord it over their subjects and make that appear good by calling themselves "benefactors." They exercise their power and try (more or less successfully) to make people think that it is for their own good. But it should never be so in the church. There, on the contrary, the one who leads is as a slave and the one who rules is as the youngest (Lk 22:24-27). Lest this lose its impact, you should stop to reflect that the youngest and the slaves are precisely those without authority in our normal sense of the word. Yet this is what leadership among Jesus' people is like.

Unfortunately, we nearly always avoid the force of this disturbing teaching by transforming it into pious rhetoric. We style ourselves as "servants" but act just like the kings of the Gentiles in exercising authority. Yet even the kings of the Gentiles try to make their authority palatable by legitimating it with pious rhetoric; this is why they call themselves "benefactors." So how are we any different? If we are to live like Jesus' followers, we need to take seriously his insight that leaders are as children and slaves, those without authority.

The most obvious aspect of what the NT has to say about leadership and authority is its lack of interest in the subject. In all of Paul's major letters, for instance, leaders only appear in Php 1:1, and there only in passing. For the most part, he ignores them, as do the other writers. Jesus' immediate followers were strangely silent about leadership and authority. This silence, it turns out, is quite significant.

The NT uses two words which correspond to different aspects of what we mean by "authority." The first, *dunamis*, is usually (and rightly) translated as "power." This word is less important for us because though "power" may be associated with some kinds of authority, it also can exist without authority. Someone waving a gun has power over others, but that does not necessarily give them authority.

Still, it will be worthwhile to look at who has *dunamis* (power) in the NT. If you take a walk through a concordance, you will find that the following possess power: God, Jesus, the Spirit, as well as angels, demons, and "principalities and powers." Human beings, oddly, don't have power themselves; they are only energized by these other powers. The ministry of the gospel, the miracles of the apostles, and the lives of believers are all conditioned on the "power of God." Strikingly, the NT seldom, if ever, recognizes human beings with "power" in their own right–power always comes to people from elsewhere.

Things become even more interesting when we turn to the other relevant Greek word: *exousia*. This word is usually translated as "power" or "authority" and is the closest equivalent to our English word "authority." The NT's list of those who have *exousia* is essentially the same as those who have dunamis: God, Jesus, the Holy Spirit, angels and demons. But now, the list extends to humans who are not merely energized by heavenly authority but have authority themselves.

Thus, kings have authority to rule (Ro 13:1-2) and Jesus' disciples have authority over diseases and spirits (e.g., Mt 10:1). Believers have authority over the various facets of their lives – their possessions (Ac 5:4), and eating, drinking, and being married (1Co 11:10). What is striking, however, is that the NT does not say anything about one believer having authority over another. We have plenty of authority over things, and even over spirits, but never over other Christians. Considering how much energy we put into discussions of who has authority in the church, that should be surprising. Kings have authority over their subjects; Paul had authority from the high priest to persecute Christians (Ac 9:14; 26:10-12). But in the church, one believer is never spoken of as having *exousia* over another, regardless of their position or prestige. The New Testament does not say anything about one believer having authority over another. We have plenty of authority over things, even over spirits, but never over other Christians. With the exception, that is, of 2Co 10:8 and 13:10. In these texts Paul speaks of having "authority" to build up, not tear down. It seems that he, at least, has exousia over other believers. Admittedly, one has to over-interpret the texts in order to make them a real exception since in both cases this is not an authority "over" anyone but rather an authority "for" a purpose.

But even granting that this over-interpretation is plausible, the exception is hardly an exception when you take two things into account. First, by his own admission, Paul is speaking "as a fool" in this part of his letter. He avoids claiming authority over others when he speaks "soberly," so it seems unlikely that he would be pleased with us using his "foolish" speech as the only basis for claiming that church leaders have spiritual authority over other believers.

Second, the context of the letter is characterized by persuasion. The profound significance of this will become clear in due course. Paul spills a great deal of ink trying to persuade the Corinthians to listen to him. If he "had authority" over them, in the sense we usually think of it, why did he bother? Why not just give the orders and be done with it? The answer, as we will see, lies in the peculiar nature of the relationship he sees between leaders and other believers.

Before we get to that, however, we should notice that Paul seems to lack authority in our everyday sense of the word (morally legitimated power) even here where he is allegedly asserting it. This should strongly caution us, then, against thinking of leaders as having authority merely on the basis of two sentences in 2Co.

Now look at things from the other side. Rather than asking who has authority in the NT, we should ask the opposite question, "Whom should one obey?" The answer here is interesting, too. If you examine the usage of *hupakouo*, which is the Greek equivalent of "obey," you will find that we ought to obey God, the gospel (Ro 10:16), and the teaching of the apostles (Php 2:12; 2Th 3:14). Children are to obey their parents and servants their masters (Ep 6:1, 5). But are believers to obey church leaders? If they are, the NT writers studiously avoid saying so.

But what about Heb 13:17 which says "obey your leaders?" This text is interesting, because it can give us an insight into the positive side of the NT's understanding of leadership. Up to now I have emphasized the negative – that they do not have authority in our usual sense, and believers are not told to obey them. In spite of all this, the NT insists that there are leaders in a local body, that they are recognizable as such, and that their existence and ministry are important to the health of the body.

What is the positive side of this understanding of leadership? There is a clue in Heb 13:17. If you examine the verb translated "obey" in this text, you will find it to be a form of the word *peitho* which means "persuade." In the form used here it means something like "let yourself be persuaded by" or "have confidence in." That's helpful. Believers are to let themselves be persuaded by their leaders.

Leaders in the church are accorded a certain respect which lends their words more weight than they have in and of themselves. And the rest of the church should be "biased" in favor of listening to what they say. We are to allow ourselves to be persuaded by our leaders, not obeying them mindlessly but entering into discussion with them and being open to what they are saying. (By the way, now it should be clear why it was so significant that Paul's statements in 2 Co were in a context of persuasion. He was trying to persuade them to let themselves be persuaded by him.)

The other verb used in Heb 13:17 reinforces this conclusion. When the text goes on to urge people to "submit" to leaders, it does not use the garden-variety Greek word for "submit." The normal word is *hupotassomai*, which connotes something like placing oneself in an organization under another person. Thus we are sometimes told to submit to governments (Ro 13:1; Tit 3:1), to the social roles in which we find ourselves (Col 3:18; 1 Pe 2:18), and to the "powers that be" of our society (1Pe 2:13).

The word here, however, is different. It is *hupeiko*, and it occurs only here in the NT. It connotes not a structure to which one submits, but a battle after which one yields. The image is one of a serious discussion, and interchange after which one party gives way. This meshes nicely with the notion that we are to let ourselves be persuaded by leaders in the church, rather than simply submitting to them as we might to the existing powers and structures of life.

All this makes sense of the criteria for elders or overseers in the pastoral epistles. In these writings, character, not charisma or administrative ability, is the most important thing about leaders. They should be "respectable." If they are supposed to be persuaders, it makes sense that they ought preeminently to be respectable because this is the kind of person whose words we are inclined to take very seriously. The kind of respectability outlined there lends credibility to the words of leaders, and hence gives us confidence in opening ourselves to being persuaded by them.

But there is more. The persuasiveness of such leaders depends on truth. Presumably, if leaders are wrong in their judgment and yet are seriously concerned to serve, they would not be happy with someone following them in their error. A leader who has the charisma to persuade people of something untrue, and does so, is virtually demonic. To be persuaded of a lie is the worst form of bondage. Leaders in the church are bound to the truth and serve it above all in their service of others.

This necessity of serving the truth, by the way, is the reason why the NT emphasizes obeying the gospel or the apostle's teaching, rather than leaders. The trust engendered by service is dangerous if it is not coordinated with a common obedience to the truth of the gospel. If the desire for truth is not at the basis of leadership in the body, the trust which can be created by service is just another, more subtle form of power – the power we call manipulation.

Persuasion presupposes dialogue; and dialogue requires the active participation of the whole body. Our common understanding of authority isolates leaders and puts them over those who are under authority. The leadership of genuine service, however, has a natural basis in the dialogue which undergirds it. Leaders in the church have need for neither the pious rhetoric of the kings of the Gentiles nor the force which lies behind it. Rather, because they are persuaders, they can rely on dialogue as the arena and channel of their service.

So, genuine leadership in the church is based on service, truth, and trust, not authority. Leaders in the church are called by the truth to lives which are worthy of imitation, and thus respectable, and to lives of service. Such a life engenders the trust of others. Yet leaders, as well as the rest of the members of the body, are always in common subjection to the truth which is in Christ.

— Hal Miller

# *6*

# CONSENSUS GOVERNING

Why did Jesus choose the word "church" to describe His followers (Mt 16:16-18)? "Church" is the English translation of the original Greek term *ekklesia*. Outside the NT, *ekklesia* was a secular word that carried strong political overtones. There were other Greek words with religious or nonpolitical associations (like *sunagogue*) that Jesus could have used, but significantly, didn't.

## THE MODERN CHURCH

According to Webster's *New Collegiate Dictionary*, "church" is used in today's English to refer to a building for Christian worship, the clergy of a religious body, a body of religious believers (i.e. a congregation or a denomination), a public divine worship service (i.e. "goes to church every Sunday"), or the clerical profession (i.e. "considered the church as a possible career"). Whereas "church" is used to translate *ekklesia*, it is actually a transliteration of an entirely different Greek adjective (*kuriakos*) which meant "of the Lord" or "belonging to the Lord." It probably is a shortened form of some such phrase as *kuriakos doma* or *kuriakos oikos* ("the Lord's house"). Thus, *kuriakos*, as with "church," can refer to those who belong to the Lord (His people) or to the Lord's house (a church building). The Greek noun that most closely parallels in meaning the English concept of "church" is *sunagogue* ("synagogue"). Both words can refer to either God's people or the special building in which they meet. The problem with all this is that every time you see "church" in the NT, it stands for the Greek *ekklesia*. Unlike "church," *sunagogue*, or *kuriakos*, the Greek *ekklesia* never refers to a building or place of worship, and it refers to much more than just a meeting, assembly, or gathering!

## THE ORIGINAL CHURCH

Outside the NT, *ekklesia* was used almost without exception to refer to a political assembly that was regularly convened for the purpose of making decisions. According to Thayer's lexicon it was "a gathering of citizens called out from their homes into some public place" and "an assembly of the people convened at the public place of council for the purpose of deliberation." The lexicon of BAGD defines *ekklesia*

69

as an "assembly of a regularly summoned political body." In Colin Brown's *New International Dictionary of New Testament Theology*, *ekklesia*, in the time of the NT, is said to have been "clearly characterized as a political phenomenon, repeated according to certain rules and within a certain framework. It was the assembly of full citizens, functionally rooted in the constitution of the democracy, an assembly in which fundamental political and judicial decisions were taken . . . the word *ekklesia*, throughout the Greek and Hellenistic areas, always retained its reference to the assembly of the polis." In the *ekklesia*, every male citizen had "the right to speak and to propose matters for discussion" (it seems that women were not allowed to speak at all in the Greek *ekklesia*).

So why did Jesus (in Mt 16:13-20; 18:15-20) choose such a politically "loaded" word as *ekklesia* (rather than something like *sunagoge*) to describe His people and their meetings? Evidently because Jesus intended for the meetings of Christians to parallel the meetings of the Greek legislators in the sense that believers are to decide things in their meetings and in the sense that kingdom citizens could speak and propose matters for discussion. Had Jesus merely wanted to describe a gathering, he could have used *sunagoge*, *thiasos* or *eranos*. Significantly however, He chose *ekklesia*. God's people, when they meet, have a decision-making mandate. A "church" is fundamentally an assembly (or meeting) of Kingdom citizens who are authorized (and expected) to make decisions, pass judgments, and weigh issues. Though this decision making need not necessarily occur at every meeting (there aren't always issues to resolve), understanding that the church has the authority and obligation to settle things is important. Any church whose meetings focus solely on praise music and teaching, to the exclusion of grappling corporately with problems and resolving issues, may be failing to fulfill its full purpose as an *ekklesia*.

That Jesus expected decision making from the *ekklesia* is seen in Mt 16:13-20. After promising to build His *ekklesia* on the rock of Peter's revealed confession, Jesus immediately spoke of the keys of the kingdom of heaven and of binding and loosing. Keys represent the ability to open and to close something, "kingdom" is a political term, and binding and loosing involves the authority to make decisions. In Mt 18:15-20, the *ekklesia* (18:17) is obligated to render a verdict regarding a brother's alleged sin, and once again, binding and loosing authority is conferred upon the *ekklesia*. In Ac 1:15-26, Peter charged the Jerusalem church as a whole with finding a replacement for Judas. In Ac 6:1-6, the apostles looked to the church corporately to pick men to administer the church's welfare system. Ac 14:23 (marginal translation) indicates that some churches elected their own elders.  In Ac 15:1-4, the church of Antioch decided to send to Jerusalem for arbitration, and then the whole church in Jerusalem was in on the resolution of the conflict (15:4, 12, 22). Finally, Paul continued this idea in 1Co 14:29-30, where it was made clear that judgment was to be passed on prophetic revelation when "the whole *ekklesia* comes together" (14:23).

By way of balance, it is important to note that the church, in its decision making role, is judicial rather than legislative.  This is one point where the *ekklesia* of God's people is different in function from the *ekklesia* of Greek cities.  Our job is not to create law – only God can rightly do that.  Instead, our duty is to apply and enforce the law of Christ correctly as contained in the New Covenant.  Thus, church members are to be like citizen-judiciaries who meet together to deliberate and decide issues, or to render judgments (when necessary).  This form of government works tolerably well in a smaller (house) church where people love each other enough to work through any disagreements.  It is virtually impossible to operate this way in a larger (institutional) church.

SHADES OF USAGE

The word *ekklesia* ("church") was used six different ways by NT writers.  One is found in Ac 19:23-41 (esp. 19:25a, 32, 39, 41).  These occurrences of *ekklesia* (rendered "assembly," "legal assembly," and "assembly") referred to a meeting of "craftsmen" (19:24) who had been "called" (19:25) together by Demetrius into the town theater (19:31) to decide what to do about Paul (19:25-27, 38), though there was so much confusion the majority did not know why they had been summoned (19:32).  This is an example of *ekklesia* used to refer to a regularly summoned political body (in this case, silver craftsmen and those in related trades).  They convened (as a sort of trade union) to decide what to do about a damaged reputation and lost business (Ac 19:27).  As it turns out, they overstepped their jurisdiction in wanting to deal with Paul, so the city clerk suggested that the matter be settled by the "legal" *ekklesia*, Ac 19:37-39 (rather than by the trade union *ekklesia)*.

Another usage is seen in Ac 7:38 and Heb 2:12, where *ekklesia* was used to refer to the gathering of the Israelis in the desert at Mount Sinai.  There they received God's legislation through Moses and decided to abide by it (Ac 7:38; Ex 24:3-7).  Furthermore, *ekklesia* was used of gatherings of Israelis at the temple during David's time (Heb 2:12; Ps 22:22).

A third usage is found in Mt 18:17; 1Co 11:17-18; 14:4-5, 18-19,

71

23, 28, and 34-35. In these verses, *ekklesia* refers to the regularly scheduled, duly convened assembly of Christians. In Mt 18:17 they met to render a decision about sin. 1Co 11 deals with a meeting of the *ekklesia* to eat the Lord's Supper, and 1Co 14 concerns the gathering of the *ekklesia* for open discussion (with edification as the chief objective).

The fourth way it is used is seen in Ac 8:1; Ro 16:1; 1Th 1:1 and Re 2:1, 8, 12, 18. Here *ekklesia* apparently is used to refer not to a meeting per se, but rather the totality of Christians living at one place. NT authors wrote of the one "church" (singular) in Jerusalem, one in Rome, one in Thessalonica, one in Ephesus, one in Smyrna, one in Pergamum, etc. However, the "church" in any given city may never have assembled together all in one place. The word "church" was used for the totality of believers in a city, but not necessarily to some massive, city wide meeting. Thus, there is only one church in Atlanta today (only one totality of Christians in Atlanta). However, the church in Atlanta will probably never be able to hold a plenary meeting (though perhaps it could have back in the 1840s when it was small). The one church in Atlanta is made up of hundreds of smaller churches that meet separately. (One church that did manage to conduct a plenary (city-wide) session was the Jerusalem church (Ac 15:12, 22).

Usage number five occurs in Ro 16:5; 1Co 16:19; Col 4:15; Phm 2. As evidenced in these texts, *ekklesia* can refer to assemblies that regularly convened in a member's home. These house churches, when considered as a whole, constituted the one city church in which they were located; though they may never have all met together.

Finally, in Mt 16:18; Ac 9:31; Ep 1:22; 3:10, 20-21; 5:23, 25-27, 29, 32, and Col 1:18; 24, *ekklesia* references the totality of Christians in all places and throughout all times (the universal church). A meeting of this universal church will not occur until the second coming of Jesus.

### APPLICATION

The word *ekklesia* is thus used six different ways in the NT. The most fundamental usage is that of a group of people gathered for the purpose of making decisions. In a very real sense, the *ekklesia* is not the coming together of God's people, it is what occurs when God's people come together. We are authorized by the Lord to make decisions about the correct application of Scripture. We are expected by the Lord to enforce the law of Christ (within the family of God) and to deal with issues as they arise. This is a part of what is to occur in our open, participatory church meetings. Problems must not be swept under the rug. Questions of correct conduct must be resolved. Of course, there will not be issues on the docket every week (or even most weeks), but God's people must ever bear in mind their obligation to function as an *ekklesia* when necessary.

This understanding of the full meaning behind *ekklesia* has a direct bearing on church government. In its human organization, the church is not supposed to be a pyramid with power concentrated at the top in one or a few men. Decisions are not to be made behind closed doors and then handed down from on high for the church to follow. The church is rather like the senate or a congress in the sense that the assembly as a whole is to deliberate upon and decide issues. The church's leaders are to facilitate this process and to serve the church by providing needed teaching and advice, but they are not the church's lords!

## CONSENSUS OR MAJORITY RULE?

The word "consensus" means "general agreement, representative trend or opinion." It is related to the word "consent" or "consensual". Majority rule can be a 51% dictatorship and often tends to work against unity. Consensus works toward unity. Taken as a principle, what do the following texts imply about majority rule (democracy) versus consensus in decision making?

"How good and pleasant it is when brothers live together in unity" (Ps 133:1).

"I appeal to you, brothers, in the name of our Lord Jesus Christ, that all of you agree with one another so that there may be no divisions among you and that you may be perfectly united in mind and thought" (1Co 1:10).

"Consequently, you are . . . members of God's household, built on the foundation of the apostles and the prophets, with Christ Jesus himself as the chief cornerstone. In him the whole building is joined together and rises to become a holy temple in the Lord. And in him you too are being built together to become a dwelling in which God lives by his Spirit" (Ep 2:19-22).

"Make every effort to keep the unity of the Spirit through the bond of peace. There is one body and one Spirit - just as you were called to one hope when you were called - one Lord, one faith, one baptism; one God and Father of all, who is over all and through all and in all" (Ep 4:3-6).

"If you have any encouragement from being united with Christ, if any comfort from his love, if any fellowship with the Spirit, if any tenderness and compassion, then make my joy complete by being like-minded, having the same love, being one in spirit and purpose" (Php 2:1-2).

"Therefore, as God's chosen people, holy and dearly loved, clothe yourselves with compassion, kindness, humility, gentleness and patience. Bear with each other and forgive whatever grievances you may have against one another. Forgive as the Lord forgave you. And over all these virtues put on love, which binds them all together in perfect unity" (Col 3:12-15).

## GOD'S PROVISION

Lest government by consensus seem too utopian, consider what the Lord has done to help His people achieve unity. First, it is important to remember that the process a church goes through in achieving consensus is often just as important as the consensus that is finally achieved. It takes time, commitment, mutual-edification, and a lot of brotherly love. It truly can work in a small, house sized church. We must love each other enough to put up with each other! Another word for consensus might be unity, oneness, harmony, or mutual agreement. Do we really trust in the Holy Spirit to work in our lives and churches?

Next, our Lord Himself prayed for His church "that they may be one as we are one . . . My prayer is . . . that all of them may be one, Father, just as you are in me and I am in you . . . May they be brought into complete unity to let the world know that you sent me and have loved them even as you have loved me" (Jn 17:11, 20-23). Since Jesus prayed this for us, unity is certainly achievable.

Another provision God made for us lies in the Lord's Supper. According to 1Co 10:17, "Because there is one loaf, we, who are many, are one body, for we all partake of the one loaf." Evidently, properly partaking of the one loaf during the Lord's Supper not only pictures unity, it can even create it!

Finally, as already mentioned above, Christ gave various ministry and leadership gifts to the church (such as apostles, prophets, evangelists, and pastor-teachers), "until we all reach unity in the faith and in the knowledge of the Son of God and become mature, attaining to the whole measure of the fullness of Christ" (Ep 4:11-13). Leaders are needed to help the church achieve consensus.

— Steve Atkerson

*Special thanks to Tim Wilson of Gig Harbor, Oregon, who first introduced me to the truth of the church as a decision making body.*

# 7

# HOUSE CHURCHES

PART ONE

Where we meet is very important. It is, of course, not as important as the living stones that are being plastered together as the church, but it is still important. I am fascinated by how often people who think like we do on many different points, will balk at my emphasis on meeting in the house. Why is this?

One reason, I think, is super-spirituality. Let the organized church worry about buildings, these folks say, but we're going to worry about building the body of Christ, and we can do that anywhere, in any building. This sounds good, but it is entirely unrealistic.

Architects and business consultants have realized for a long time that buildings and their accouterments will affect people's moods and relationships. One thinks of the proverbial banker's desk and visitor's chair. When you sit in the chair, the desk is about neck-high, and you feel very small and very inferior to the banker. Take another example: suppose you want to have close, intimate communion with your brothers and sisters. You go to a church building. You put the chairs in a circle. You're still faced with the open spaces that kill intimacy, and make it hard to hear. You've got cold fluorescent lights overhead. And you've got decades of acculturation to deal with. When you're in a building, you're used to thinking institutionally and formally.

Let me quote from a critic who believes in church life, but who thinks the building in which the church meets is not important: "I do not believe that the answer lies in forsaking 'church buildings' in favor of 'living rooms.' Nor are sweat shirts and jeans inherently more conducive to effective fellowship and ministry than three piece suits and neckties. It seems to me that such proposals merely exchange one external 'hang-up' for another. To prove that there were no 'church buildings' in the first few decades of the church's existence is to prove nothing. There were also no automobiles, or telephones, or computers, or printing presses . . . Should we also view these advances as detrimental to church life? Or does the real problem actually lie in the way we use these tools? If a church 'building' is worshiped more than the One in whose name we gather, something has certainly gone wrong. If such is the case, selling the building and crowding into a living room will do little to solve the problem. What is needed is a change of heart and mind, not of location and surroundings . . . It is just as easy to spawn and perpetuate false teaching, factionalism, groundless ritual, and stifling traditions in a living room as it is in a 'church building.' And one can be deliberately ostentatious in ragged jeans and worn-out Reeboks as in a well pressed suit and polished wingtips."

Let's examine one by one the propositions set forth above. The first is, "I do not believe that the answer lies in forsaking 'church buildings' in favor of 'living rooms'." This is a half-truth, and like all half-truths, it is entirely misleading. Of course, exchanging church buildings in favor of living rooms is not the whole answer. It is however, part of the answer. In fact, it is a necessary part of the answer (although it is not sufficient in and of itself). More on this later.

His second proposition is, "Sweat shirts and jeans are not inherently more conducive to fellowship and ministry than three piece suits and neckties." At this point, you will have to excuse me. Heretofore, I have been measured, rational, and moderate. But I refuse to be measured, rational, and moderate when one tries to defend neckties. Ladies and gentlemen, if you want to grab hold of a piece of wisdom that will bless you for the rest of your life, please listen to this truth: neckties are of the devil! (I, of course, jest here). I know a brother who calls a necktie a "choking spirit." I sometimes suspect that he is right. The problem is not merely that the thing is so utterly useless; rather, a necktie is a positive evil relative to church life. It's very purpose is to choke off intimacy, and establish formality. It is actually written in the code of ethics for lawyers that they have to wear "appropriate" dress, so as not to bring disrepute on the profession. Have you ever seen a lawyer at work without a necktie? The purpose is to establish professionalism. The purpose is to make you think that he is competent, intelligent, and important. It's purpose is not to make you more intimate with him. How many people do you know that insist on wearing a tie to church, then go home and wear one? They don't. Why not? Because they are with their family, and they don't need to be formal with their family. Why do Christians need to be formal with their brothers and sisters? I know of many churches which started wonderfully, and then began to institutionalize. It is inevitable that at some point along the way, the leaders will be told they must wear ties. It is at this point that you may be certain the church has died, just as you know a patient has died when his EKG shows no brain waves.

A third point is, "To prove that there were no church buildings in the early church is to prove nothing. There were also no automobiles, or telephones, or computers, or printing presses." And, of course, as this old argument runs, there is nothing wrong with cars or phones, they are morally neutral, they can be used for good as well as bad, and so can church buildings. This argument has a surface validity, but it is fallacious. A church building is often not "morally neutral." It is not an adventitious piece of technology that can be used for good or evil. If church buildings are not important, why have Christians sunk 180 billion dollars into building them? If you don't think they are important, go ask a traditional church pastor to sell his church building and give the money to the poor in the name of Jesus, and see what kind of response you'll get. Of all the money Christians faithfully put in the plate, how much of it goes to the gospel, or to the needy, and how much goes to the parking lots, the steeples, the carpets? How many church splits are generated by disputes over the color of carpets, the placement of church furniture, and other momentous issues? Everyone reading this knows as well as I do that the church building today is typically nothing more than a holy shrine, a phony substitute temple for the true temple of God, which is the body of Christ. People don't fight over computers, automobiles, telephones, and printing presses. But they will fight over a church building. Why? Because the church building can easily become an idolatrous object of worship.

His fourth statement is that "What is needed is a change of heart and mind, not of location and surroundings." This argument is one whose foundation rests in super-spirituality. It would work if human beings were airy wraiths who floated through life totally unaffected by their grubby material surroundings. But unfortunately, we humans are very much influenced by our surroundings. Lets take this argument to its logical extreme. Suppose you had a brother who was destitute, jobless, homeless, and miserable. Would you tell him, "Brother, what you need is a change of heart and mind, not a change of location and surroundings!"?

We cannot divorce our attitudes and assumptions from the environmental influences which shape us from a very young age. Thus, if a child attends church his whole life in a church building, he or she will wind up later in life thinking that church buildings hold a holy position in God's eyes as the appropriate place to meet. To say that we should examine our hearts before we examine our church buildings ignores the reciprocal influence that each has on the other.

A fifth assertion the critic is that, "It is just as easy to spawn and perpetuate false teaching, factionalism, groundless ritual, and stifling traditions in a living room as it is in a 'church building'." This is not true. Although false teaching, factionalism, groundless ritual, etc. can easily be spawned in a house, it is not true that they can easily be perpetuated in a living room. Why? Because it takes the living Christ dwelling inside people to keep the church alive without bureaucracy, ritual, and building. And as soon as the life of Christ is replaced by fleshly substitutes, the house church dies, because there is not bureaucracy, ritual, and building to keep it perpetuated. In fact, as human flesh moves in on a house church, you will begin to hear calls for one or more of three things: imported pastors, buildings, and neckties. Why the call for a building? Because human flesh loves illusions of permanence, beauty, and protection. And if Jesus isn't providing those things, fleshly religious people are going to instinctively look to a building for a substitute. This is not to blame the death and fleshiness on the building, but it is to say that the building is the outward sign of the death and fleshiness that is within.

While we're on the subject of church buildings, lets talk about the furniture inside of church buildings. For instance, they line you up so you can fellowship with the back of your brother's or sister's head. Pews don't promote intimacy, but rather cold formality. They also cost a small fortune. Pulpits (lecterns) came from Martin Luther. Luther had been given control of formerly Catholic cathedrals. He was preaching in one of them, needed a place to prop his notes, looked up and saw on a pillar the little rostrum or pulpit that the Catholic priest had climbed up to in order to read weekly announcements. Luther ripped out the old Catholic altar, and replaced it with the Protestant pulpit. This is used today to make the person standing behind it feel big and important. It is made to awe you, the humble pew-sitter, to keep you from asking questions, and from falling asleep. Its very presence is intimidating to dialogue, communication, and sharing. An altar in the OT is a place where a sacrifice was slain. The OT foreshadowed the sacrifice of Jesus in the NT, so it seems to me that the only "altar" in the NT is the cross, upon which Jesus was slain. This, however, does not stop the very many institutional churches who put little padded benches up front and call them "altars." But, even if they are called "prayer benches," or something similar, they still reinforce the idea that there's something going on up front apart from the audience. The altar is just one more piece of religious furniture that reinforces spectator Christianity, the kind that Watchman Nee said engenders "passivity and death."

So far this critique of church buildings has focused on two main points: their obscene and wasted expense, and their frequent use as idolatrous substitutes for the worship of Christ. However, there are other reasons we should avoid church buildings like the plague. One reason is that buildings are harmful to church life because they permit the church to grow to such a size that it is impossible to have intimate fellowship anymore. How many times have you heard Christians say, "This was a wonderful church back in the old days when we were small, but now we don't know anybody." A house church can never grow that large, because not everyone can fit in the living room. (Which means, incidentally, that for house churches to grow, they must divide and multiply.)

Another reason is that certain normative NT practices can't be accomplished easily in a large church setting. For example, weekly partaking of the Lord's Supper, taking of the Lord's Supper with one loaf and one cup, partaking of the Lord's Feast, and mutual participation and sharing are easily handled in a house church setting, but not so in larger institutional churches.

A third reason not to have a special building is the total absence in the New Testament of instructions to construct such buildings. If we obey the commandment in De 12:32, we must not add to God's word. It is only logical to assume that if God wanted us to have buildings, He would have so ordered in His Word. Consider that all of the gospel and letter writers in the NT, with the exception of Luke, formerly participated in temple worship. It is highly significant that not one of them ever built or instructed anyone to build any type of Christian building. This includes Paul, Peter, and John. The absence of special buildings in the NT is noteworthy to say the least.

Finally, it has never been the way of God to extend His witness through a building made with the hands of human beings! His method of extending his witness is through the flesh, blood, and bones of the believing body of Jesus Christ, and not a building. The entire book of Acts verifies this doctrinal truth. How much it must grieve the heart of God to watch His body operate in the unsuccessful Jewish method of witness extension: confining the primary energies, ministries, and vision of God to a building. God's commission to His church is to go to the lost in their environment, not invite them into an edifice! We must get out of this inwardly focused building mentality and into real ministry.

— Dan Trotter

PART TWO

Why do we keep insisting that churches ought to meet in people's houses? Won't anywhere else do? A lot of churches that practice in the way we advocate meet in Christian book shops and coffee shops that have a lounge area just like in someone's private house; what's wrong with that? Well, I suppose that in some parts of the world Eskimos might meet in igloos and Red Indians in teepees; and of course on a nice day (and we even get them occasionally here in England too) what possible objection could there be to meeting in the garden (that's the 'yard' to my American readers) or in a field somewhere? And to the above I have no objections whatsoever, but merely wish to bring us back to the essential point that the format for church gatherings in the New Testament kept each individual church small in numbers, and was therefore simply perfectly suited to everything occurring in people's home. What more, after all, does a biblically based church need for it's gatherings than the homes of those who are part of it? And when it comes to biblical churches meeting in lounge areas of book shops and coffee shops – or indeed, in any other public building – there is actually a big problem that will (hopefully) have to eventually be faced, but of which most believers seem to be completely unaware.

Now it is certainly true that a church could meet in a public building of some kind and still remain small enough in number to function as scripture teaches; and if such a building can be arranged with a nice cozy lounge area and made to feel "like home," then all the better. Indeed, assuming there are kitchen facilities then there isn't even a problem regarding sharing the love-feast together. But there is yet another problem to be faced, and a big one too, and it is simply this: A first-generation biblical church may well be able to come together and meet in such a way without any problem - but what of the situation once growth occurs and other churches need to come into being from it? (I am assuming that, being biblically based, this imagined church does indeed want to grow numerically, as the Lord enables, and not just remain the same personnel its whole life.) So, do you see the problem? That church can't just keep getting numerically bigger (even though larger numbers can easily be accommodated by virtue of the fact of it meeting in a public building) because it could then no longer function in the way the New Testament teaches that it should, and another church needs to come into existence. And here is the point: So where will that church meet?

Now there may, of course, be an abundant supply of Christian coffee houses and book shops around with nice lounge and kitchen areas, and so I guess new churches could just go and hire them out, but I nevertheless think that an important question remains: Why not just meet in each others houses? I mean, what is the problem with simply doing that? It is, after all, what every church in scripture did. (Every time individual churches are given a location in the New Testament it is always, and without fail, in someone's home.) So why, oh why, do you want to be different? Why be a church that is biblically based in every other respect, having bought into the notion that we should do things just like they did back then, and then break ranks over this?

Could it possibly be (though surely not) that behind this is a feeling that opening our homes to each other is a bit too inconvenient? Too close for comfort, even? The apostles of Jesus taught believers to open their homes to each other and to actually have their church gatherings in each others homes too. After all, am I truly known as I should be if my home-life isn't wide open to those with whom I have fellowship? Can people know me properly, truly and deeply, if they don't regularly see my home life and family life and have it shared with them? Are we really to believe that meeting in homes was a purely incidental aspect of the blueprint for church life we find in scripture, or is it as significant and important as the other aspects such as open, participatory gatherings, having the Lord's Supper as a full meal and practicing biblical leadership consensual church government? I put it to you that the burden of proof very much lies with those who seem to think it unimportant!

However, let me say too that where homes are literally too small to have more than three or four people visiting at any one time (Tokyo, perhaps?), then by all means make other appropriate provision; but of course the irony is that the very place this trend is particularly prevalent, America, homes are very definitely on the large size. (At least they are by our standards here in England where, incidentally, at our church we pack each other into our homes, come what may, even though it means that in some of them, mine included, you can't see the carpet any more.)

So if you are a biblical church meeting in a coffee house somewhere then fine, that sure is better than being an unbiblical church meeting in someone's home, but do take on board the simple fact that, should you grow and become too large numerically to remain one church any longer (and as I have already indicated, you should most certainly desire such to be the case), then how ridiculous to be out trying to find more and more Christian coffee houses and the like rather than just locating each church's gatherings in the homes of those who are part of them. And how ridiculous as well to end up, say, with one church gathering in people's homes, whilst the original one continues to meet in the coffee house or book shop or public hall or whatever.

Whichever way you look at it, it seems quite illogical to not just do things the way the New Testament churches, under the direction of the apostles, did them. A church can indeed meet in a public building and yet remain truly biblical in every other way as far as practice is concerned, but the question remains: When it is quite feasible, all things being equal, to meet in each others homes, and given that this was the universal practice of the New Testament churches as taught and directed by the apostles of Jesus, then why on earth would any otherwise biblical church want to decide not to do likewise?

— Beresford Job

PART THREE

**How can a church keep from wearing out the host family and their home?** Some people really do have the gift of hospitality and wont mind hosting the church every week, but admittedly this can be quite taxing. This is especially a problem if one spouse is out of tune with the other. Typically, the tuned-out spouse (usually a man) will be clueless to the miseries that the other one (usually the wife) is suffering in hosting the church weekly. The solutions are many: church members could come over early to help clean up both before and after the meeting. Perhaps a better alternative is for the meeting location to be rotated on a weekly basis, with all who are able sharing the load. It is good for others to learn hospitality! Further, each home could have its own house "rules', such as: please take off your shoes when entering the house, no children jumping on the furniture, no eating in the living room, etc.

**What if the homes are tiny and just too small for a meeting?** This can be a real problem. Of course, the houses in China are small, and they still meet in them for church! One alternative is to add on to a home to make the meeting room bigger, or knock out a wall, or close in a garage. If all else fails, renting an apartment clubhouse or some similar arrangement can work, as long as the objective is not to hold more people than could fit into a moderately well to do home.

**How can we keep the neighbors from complaining about the cars?** Rotate the church meeting from week to week between different homes, park only on one side of the street, be sure to fill up the drive way to get as many cars as possible off the street, park at a nearby school or closed store, etc. Remember too that the idea is to start a new church after the existing church starts to get crowded. There should not be all that many cars pulling up!

**What type of property damage can hosting the church cause?** Spilled drinks, food dropped on upholstery, crayon markings on the floor and table cloth, tracked in mud, etc. During one home church meeting a teenage girl ran through a closed sliding glass door. Be mentally prepared for accidents.

**What if people enjoy the fellowship so much that they never go home?** Actually, this is a good problem to have! Since church is like a family, this may likely occur. Put their needs above your own. Die to self. However, if some attention starved couple lingers each week for hours after every one else has left, just explain that you have other matters to attend to and ask them to leave! People that insensitive to your needs will never get the hint unless you spell it out for them. This is part of learning how to interact with others.

**How would you handle a situation where visitor's children, or the children of a newly attending couple, are not well behaved?** Some couples' standards of acceptable social behavior are vastly different from others' standards. It may shock and amaze you at how indifferent some parents are to the destructive actions of their children. In such cases you must calmly, politely, and directly ask them to control their children! And, expect them to be offended no matter how tactfully you approach them. That is just the way it is. Count on this: it will happen. (A helpful book to have on hand to give out is, *To Train Up A Child*, by Michael Pearl. Order it from www.NoGreaterJoy.Org).

Home meetings are not easier, but they are the NT way!

— Steve Atkerson

# 8

# CHILDREN IN CHURCH

At a Virginia house church conference, before a panel discussion was about to begin, I whispered to a friend that I bet the first question was going to be: "How do we handle the children?" Sure enough, it was. This, in my opinion, is the number one question asked by those contemplating the house church. It is a tremendous stumbling block, but it shouldn't be. This chapter will examine three things: first, the differing philosophies or mind sets that the institutional and house church have toward children and the church; second, practical issues that arise; and third, the advantage to children of the church in the home.

In an article I once wrote, I asked the question: "What do you do *for* the children?" I am ashamed to say that the first draft of that article read: "What do you do *with* the children?" I had subconsciously succumbed to the philosophy or mind set of much of the institutional church: children are a problem, they interfere with the almighty "service," where important, paid professionals in robes or coats and ties give important speeches, and where serious, quiet, and holy listeners sit deathly still in pews. So, the question becomes, what do we do with the children while we are doing the important things in the "service"?

Neither Jesus, nor the apostles, ever worried about what to do with the children. Jesus never, ever said: "Suffer the little children to be packed away in the nursery." Can you imagine the children being led to Children's Church during the Sermon on the Mount?

The Scripture doesn't say much on handling children when believers gather. But I can't imagine that the believers back then didn't have children. I imagine not much was ever said, because the early Christians didn't make such a big deal about the issue. The churches were in the home; families lived in homes; children met with the church in the home.

Although the scriptures don't say anything directly concerning the children and the gatherings of believers, there are glimpses. For example, children are explicitly stated to have been present at the feeding of the five thousand, and the feeding of the four thousand (Mt 14:21, 14:38.). On a missionary journey, "all the disciples and their wives and *children"* accompanied the apostles, as they left, to pray on the beach (Ac 21:5b). Finally, when Paul's letter was read to the Ephesians, it addresses the children directly: "children, obey your parents in the Lord" (Ep 6:1-2). How could the children hear that exhortation read in church, unless the children were in the church meeting?

And despite the relative Scriptural silence on kids and church, I can guarantee one thing: there weren't any Sunday Schools and Children's Churches. If Sunday Schools are essential adjuncts to church life, why is the Bible silent on this subject? His building plan, the Bible, is complete in every detail. Where is the Christian who would deny that the Bible is a perfect blueprint? Interestingly, there is not even a hint of Sunday Schools in God's blueprint.

Sunday Schools were not even originated to teach Bible stories or Christian morality, but were started in nineteenth century England to give poor children of mill and mine laborers a chance to read and write. Who had primary responsibility for training children before the appearance of Sunday Schools? The family. I think it is the contention of most house churches that the family still has the primary responsibility for the instruction and nurturing of Christian children. That may be the reason most home churches (just like the biblical NT church) don't have Sunday Schools. And this really is a barrier to Christians who contemplate leaving the institutional church for the home church. It is amazing how many Christians worry about the spiritual welfare of their kids to the point that the parents will poison themselves to death on the corrupt religiosity of some institutional churches, just so long as there's a good youth program. I am convinced that many institutional churches realize this, and capitalize on it by providing jam-up "youth ministries," in order to keep their "tithe-payers" from leaving (of course, I realize that often there are other, sincere motives involved, too).

Although it is the family's primary duty to raise children up in the Lord, it does not follow that the home church should be uninterested in their welfare. Quite the contrary. If kids see their parents' church as a drag, they'll tend to think Jesus is a drag, too. Thus we must discuss practical ways for the home church to make children know that the church belongs to them as well as to their parents.

In discussing practical ways to integrate children into the life of the home church, we must understand at the onset that if parents bring the traditional mind set of the institutional church into the house church, nothing will work for the kids. The institutional church has the mentality of juvenile segregation: push them out into the Sunday School wing, so everything can be Holy and Quiet. This, of course, is unbiblical. How quiet do you think the kids were during the Sermon on the Mount? The institutional church is liturgically rigid in its "order of service," and kids, being as unprogrammed and unpredictable as they are, can never fit within that rigidity. So the first practical thing to do in the church in the home is to relax – there's going to be more noise and interruption in the house church. People with children need to quit feeling guilty about it, and people without children need to exercise more tolerance than they would in the institutional church.

The second practical thing to do is to develop close relationships between each adult, and between all adults and all children. This development is possible in the home church, in a way that it is not possible in the organized church. With close relationships, when little Johnny is about to flush the cherry bomb down the toilet, an adult who is not Johnny's parent can firmly request that the little hellion extinguish the wick, without fear of alienating little Johnny or little Johnny's mom. Close relationships are extremely important.

The third practical thing that should be done is to find creative, workable ways to involve the kids in the meeting with the adults. Where did the idea come from that the meeting (or the church) belongs exclusively to the adults? I know of one house church in which the children are generally musically gifted. The young folks play guitars, violins, and flutes, and feel free to lead out in song or music. Other home churches encourage kids to share testimonies, or to recite memorized scripture, or to ask for prayer requests. During one meeting, my particular home church allowed the teenage young people to lead the meeting with Scripture and music. The meeting was entirely different – it gave us variety, and helped the young people join in. During another meeting in my home church, one of the sisters conducted a "Sunday School lesson" for the young children with the adults present. The adults were forced to adapt to a young child's viewpoint (something that all adults should do periodically), and the kids were able to have fun with their parents as they learned the spiritual lesson being taught.

The fourth practical thing I would suggest is not to be hidebound by "house church theology." Sure, we don't believe in Sunday Schools, but the world's not going to end if someone has something special for the kids, or if he takes them aside in another room once in a while. And we don't believe in pacifying the kids with entertainment to keep them out of our hair, but there's nothing wrong with showing them a video once in a while (even, heaven forbid, if the video is a Bugs Bunny cartoon, and not spiritual).

A fifth practical suggestion that one house churcher has suggested is for each meeting home to have announced house rules, so that children and parents might not inadvertently harm anything (for instance, "no eating in the living room.").

A sixth practical suggestion is to tolerate fussing infants as much as you can, but if they get too loud, make sure the parents understand that the baby should be taken out of the meeting until he cools off. If a parent doesn't do this, the parent should be communicated with. Remember, relationships are important. We need to constantly put ourselves in the shoes of our brothers and sisters – and our kids are, in the body of Christ, our brothers and sisters. Let's prefer them in love. (A great book to supply to parents whose children are out of control is *To Train Up A Child*, by Michael & Debi Pearl. Order from www.NoGreaterJoy.org).

My seventh, and last, practical suggestion, is never to let the meeting become boring – neither for the children, nor for the adults. If the meeting is dead or too long for the adults, imagine what its like for the kids! Their attention span is probably about half of ours. We need to constantly put ourselves in the shoes of our brothers and sisters – and our kids are, in the body of Christ, our brothers and sisters. Let's prefer them in love.

We finish these thoughts on children and the house church by presenting the manifest advantages of the home church for young folks. We should not look upon children as an obstacle to getting folks into the house church. We should look at the advantages of the house church for kids, and point out these advantages to potential house church converts.

One big advantage of the home church for young people is that the youth get to see their parents in loving, supportive relationships with one another. They get to see their parents open their hearts to God in a real, personal, nonreligious, un-phony fashion.

Another tremendous advantage is that the kids are not given second-class status in the church: they are not segregated, put out of sight, out of mind in nurseries, Sunday Schools, and youth ministries.

One of the biggest advantages, in my view, is the close relationships that develop between adults and children of other adults. In my home church, I constantly pray for the children involved. There are only six couples in the church, and only fourteen children. It's very easy to find out what's going on in the kid's lives, and easy to pray for them daily, individually, by name. I submit to you that this doesn't happen very often in the mega-church.

CONCLUSION

I close my chapter on children in church with a brilliant piece by Doug Phillips of Vision Forum on his church's Youth Program. Although he is describing a church that is clearly not living-room sized, his points are still quite relevant:

"I have the privilege of worshiping in a small, family-integrated church. When asked about our various church programs, I explain that we are blessed with more than thirty different organizations to which our members belong - they are called families. I further explain that we have more than sixty youth directors - they are called parents. In fact, we have such a full schedule of events that there is a mandatory activity every day of the week - it is called family worship.

Both through the preaching of the word and informal shepherding of the congregation, the church leadership aspires to equip our dozens and dozens of youth pastors to successfully minister to the diverse needs of the many individuals and special interest groups within their respective organizations. Because we don't want to leave anybody behind, we have instructed these church organizations to reach out to the young, the old, and the infirm - the singles, the divorced, or abandoned - everybody, such that we will have a comprehensive outreach for every special interest group represented by the membership of our assembly of believers. As a result, these organizations sponsor events that include hospitality and evangelism outreach, one-room schoolhouses (usually meeting in the family den), foreign missions (to Mexico), and literally hundreds of other activities designed to meet the needs of the organizational members.

The amazing thing is that our financial budget to accomplish these goals is $0.00. Well, that is not exactly true - we do spend some money on photocopying, tape distribution, and various other training tools that we place in the hands of our youth directors.

As an example to the congregation, the elders are required to be youth directors, too. In fact, if the elders don't manage their own youth programs well, they have to step down from being elders.

With so much responsibility on their hands, our youth directors have to really get their collective acts together. (I happen to be one of the youth directors, so I speak from personal experience.) They have to study God's Word more than they have ever studied before so they can wisely lead their organization. They have to be creative so they can solve the diverse problems of their special interest groups. They have to learn to be patient. They have to learn to love. They even have to reprioritize their lives.

This last part is crucial. Only by reprioritizing life, and structuring their organizations properly, will our youth directors be successful. They know that. They also know there is a price to pay. But most of them are willing to pay the price, because they have decided that the greatest activity they can do in this life is to be a youth pastor and to run a special interest organization called the Christian family.

Here is what we are discovering: The more we commit to faithfully shepherding our mini-congregations, the more blessing we experience. Moreover, the more we study what God's Word says about these little congregations, the more we see the wonder and the brilliance of God's plan of equipping the Church and transforming the entire culture through these often forgotten, twisted, and even maligned organizations called Christian households."

— Dan Trotter

### VIEW POINT NUMBER ONE

If you ever wish to see a gathering Evangelicals gnash their teeth and rend their garments as in olden times, all you have to do is stand before them and quote with enthusiasm, "women should remain silent in the churches" (1Co 14:34)! If you manage to survive the ensuing stoning, you will also be accosted with a combination of incredulous questioning and outraged challenges. On several occasions I have seen brothers verbally pilloried for merely reading 1Co 14:33-35 in the course of attempting to teach through 1Co 14 in general. Correctly explaining and applying this passage that seems to require silence of a woman in a church meeting is thus a challenge, not only because of its exegetical difficulties, but also because of the explosive nature of the topic. The entire quote (NIV) reads, "As in all the congregations of the saints, women should remain silent in the churches. They are not allowed to speak, but must be in submission, as the Law says. If they want to inquire about something, they should ask their own husbands at home; for it is disgraceful for a woman to speak in the church."

**1. The command *seems* clear.** This one paragraph states four different ways that women are not to address the church:

A. "women should remain silent in the churches"
B. "they are not allowed to speak"
C. "they should ask their husbands at home"
D. "it is a disgrace for a woman to speak in the church"

1Co 11a makes it plain that women are legitimately able to pray and prophesy. An important question concerns where that prayer and prophecy is to occur. May it be expressed in the gathering of the whole church on the Lord's Day? Those who understand the prayer and prophecy by women in 1Co 11 to have occurred in a church meeting obviously are forced to reject a face value requirement of women's silence in 1Co 14. On the other hand, if the prayer and prophecy of 1Co 11 occurred informally, apart from a church meeting, then a face value application of 1Co 14 would become a more legitimate option. The evidence for the setting of 1Co 11a will be considered below. However, whatever the setting of 1Co 11a, it should be clearly observed that God was pleased to gift certain women with the gift of prophecy (Joel

2:28ff, Ac 2). Further, it is a fair statement that our sisters' prayers are as important to God as are any brother's.

**2. It applies to "all" churches.** That women were "silent" in all first century church meetings everywhere (and not just Corinth) is evident from the way the paragraph begins, "As in all the churches of the saints, women should remain silent in the churches" (14:33b). Further, the Greek tense behind "should remain silent" is a present imperative, which generally commands the continuation of an existing condition ("keep on remaining silent")*. Thus we see that the women in both Corinth, and all the other churches, were already silent. This was not a new command; they were merely being confirmed in what they were already doing. *This is a grammatical fact recognized in even basic Greek books (*Beginner's Grammar of the Greek New Testament*, New York: Harper & Row, Publishers, W.H. Davis, p. 168).

The New Covenant brought new freedom and liberty not found in the Old Covenant. For instance, rather than just male Levite priests, now all believers, men and women, are priests. Rather than just Hebrews being God's people, under the New Covenant all believers, Jew and Gentile alike, are God's people. Rather than special dietary restrictions, now all food is clean. The Corinthians had written Paul many questions (7:1) about our new liberties in Christ. It appears as if some in Corinth had also questioned the proper role of the sisters in a church meeting. This letter to the Corinthians is his response to their queries.

**3. "Women" (sisters) may not be "brothers."** In many contexts the word "brothers" refers to both men and women. Other times, it refers only to believing men (as in 1Co 7:29, 9:5). Some argue that throughout the letter to the Corinthians, "brothers" refers to both men and women. Is this the case also in 1Co 14? Sailing into chapter 14, having begun in chapter 1, the flow would seem to indicate so. The readers, throughout 1Co 14, are addressed as either "brothers" or "you" (2nd person pronoun). However, there is a significant and unexpected pronoun shift from "you" to "they" (3rd person pronoun) in the paragraph concerning women (14:33b-35). Rather than writing, "women . . .you", the text states, "women . . . they." Why did Paul not write directly to the sisters, if they were included in the term "brothers"?

This pronoun shift can be easily accounted for if the word "brothers" throughout 1Co 14 actually refers primarily to the men. The women would thus be referred to in 3rd person, since they are written about, rather than directly addressed. So, when it is stated that "all", "anyone", or "each one" of the "brothers" can participate in the interactive meeting (14:26), it may be specifically the men who are referred to.

The women ("they") are not to make comments designed for the whole church to hear. Interestingly, the *textus receptus* adds the word "your" before "women" in 14:34, further evidence that the term "brothers" throughout 1Co 14 specifically referred to the men and not the women. Since Paul had no hesitation about addressing women directly in other of his letters (for instance Euodia and Syntyche in Php 4:2), the fact that he did not here, in 1Co 14, makes the case above all the more compelling.

Gordon Fee, in his commenary on this passage, observed, "all the previous directions given by the apostle, including the inclusive 'each one' of v. 26 and the 'all' of v. 31, were *not* to be understood as including women." (Fee also goes on to attempt to prove that 1Co 14:34-35 is a scribal gloss of unauthentic origin, p. 706, *New International Commentary on the New Testament: The First Epistle To The Corinthians*, Grand Rapids: Eerdmans Publishing).

Looking at this another way, perhaps the sisters were indeed included in the word, "brothers." Consider the case of a man gifted with tongues. He would obviously be counted among the "brothers" referred to in 1Co 14. Further, in 1Co 14:26, "everyone" of the "brothers" is said to be able to contribute a "tongue". Reading this, the tongue-speaking brother would anticipate the free exercise of his gift. Yet, in 14:28, the tongue speaker is informed that if no interpreter is present, he must keep silent and not speak in tongues. The chapter is still written to and for him, and the truth of interactive meetings still applies, but his participation in the meeting is limited. The same would hold true for the prophet (if a revelation comes to another, the first prophet should stop). Would God give a prophet a prophecy that the prophet was not free to deliver? Evidently so, based on the inspired text ("the first speaker should stop" and "the spirits of prophets are subject to the control of prophets"). Finally, the same would apply to the women also, even if they are counted among the "brothers", who subsequently learn in 14:33b-35 that they are not to speak to the church either.

**4. "Silent" really does mean silent.** The word divinely chosen for "silent" is *sigao*, defined in BAGD's *Lexicon* as "be silent, keep still, say nothing." There exists a much less harsh term, *hesuchia*, which primarily means "quiet" in the sense of tranquil (1Ti 2:11-12). Significantly, however, *hesuchia* is not used here. The women were to be silent (*sigao*) with respect to speaking during the 1Co 14 meeting.

**5. The silence is limited to solo speaking.** The same Greek word translated "silent" (*sigao*) in 14:34 is also used with reference to the tongues speakers (14:28) and prophets (14:30). Each time *sigao* is used in 1Co 14, it is carefully qualified (limited in scope). So too with the women's silence: it is qualified by the word "speak." The Holy Spirit easily could have added, "they are not permitted to speak in judgment of prophecies," or "they are not permitted to speak a teaching," but instead He said, "they are not permitted to speak." Thus, women are to remain silent with respect to speaking in the church meeting. The context is clear about what is being regulated: situations where only one person is up addressing the whole church ("one at a time", 14:27 & "in turn", 14:31). The silence requirement would therefore not apply to women singing in congregation, whispered comments not intended for the whole church, laughing, playing an instrument, etc.

Again quoting Fee, "Despite protests to the contrary, the 'rule' itself is expressed absolutely. That is, it is given without any form of qualification. Given the unqualified nature of the further prohibition that 'the women' are not permitted to speak, it is very difficult to interpret this as meaning anything else than all forms of speaking out in public . . . the plain sense of the sentence is an absolute prohibition of all speaking in the assembly." (p. 706-707).

**6. "Speak" refers to public statements.** From *laleo*, "speak" is used throughout 1Co 14 primarily with reference to those who would *laleo* publicly to the assembled church (with a hymn, a teaching, an interpretation, etc.). In fact, the solution for a would-be public tongue speaker (with no interpreter present) is for him to instead *laleo* privately to himself and to God (14:28). Such private *laleo* is encouraged, not condemned. Thus the regulations throughout 1Co 14 primarily concern instances of public *laleo* , not private *laleo*. Similarly, Paul is not here prohibiting private *laleo* (conversation) between two women in 14:33b-35, but rather public *laleo*. Thus in this context, *laleo* (14:34) does not likely refer primarily to idle, thoughtless private babble nor to inconsiderate and distracting private chatting (though such would also be inappropriate). Instead, that which is being prohibited is public speaking intended for the whole church to hear.

**7. Silence is an act of submission.** "They are not allowed to speak, but must be in submission" (14:34). For a woman to teach, judge a prophecy or dispute with a teacher would clearly not be speaking from a position of submission. Indeed, such is expressly prohibited in 1Ti 2:11-12. However, the inspired text goes even further in 1Co 14, and associates public speaking by a woman in a church meeting as an insubmissive activity. Head coverings, in 1Co 11a, are said to be a "sign" of submission to authority. Silence, in 1Co 14, is said to be an actual form of submission.

**8. Submission is an Old Testament principle.** An appeal is made for the women to be submissive "as the Law says" (14:34). The word "Law" can refer not only to Mosaic legislation, but also to the entirety of the Hebrew Scriptures. It is so used here. The silence of women is not what the Law teaches. However, as is clear from the tenor of the Hebrew Scriptures, starting with creation, women are to be submissive to their husbands. Men were the leaders in both Hebrew society and religion (e.g., only men could be priests, the vast majority of the prophets were male, all the writing prophets were men, in the few historical examples where women did prophesy to men they did so in a more private setting, most of the political leaders were men, families were patriarchal, vows made by a wife could be revoked by her husband, Deborah rebuked Barak for wanting a woman to help him lead, etc.). Thus, the submission of the women, as expressed in 1Co 14 by their silence, is consistent with God's truth revealed throughout the Old Testament.

**9. Even inquiries are prohibited.** Asking a question is the opposite of making a statement, yet even this is declared to be out of order in 14:35. Instead, women should "ask their own husbands at home." Why? Because "it is disgraceful for a woman to speak in the church" (14:35). If Paul, under the inspiration of the Holy Spirit, declares a certain activity to be "disgraceful", then it is as if Christ Himself were declaring it to be disgraceful. Ultimately, how do we know what pleases our Lord unless He tells us? In God's household, it evidently is disgraceful for a woman to speak to the gathering of the church.

During the outpouring of the Spirit at Pentecost, both men and women prophesied and supernaturally spoke in other languages. This resulted in a great number of conversions as people heard the gospel in their own language. Women may pray in prayer meetings, and speak or prophesy at evangelistic events. However, during the regular, weekly, Lord's Day meetings of the whole church they evidently are not to speak.

**10. "Disgrace" (14:35) does not mean "obscene."** In an apparent effort to make a face value reading of the command for silence to appear improbable, some have suggested that the proper translation here should be "obscene." They then cry, "Our sister's voices are not obscene!" The simple fact is that the Greek underlying "disgrace" (1Co 14: 35) does not mean "obscene." "Obscene" is too strong a word. "Disgrace" is from *aischros* (#150), defined by the lexicon as "shame, ugly, base." *Aischros* is used other places in the Bible with reference to dishonest gain (Tit 1:11), of women with short hair and of men with long hair (1Co 11:6). I could not find a lexicon that suggested it funda-

95

mentally means "obscene." In essence, those who say such erect and knock over a straw man in an attempt to make this biblical command seem ridiculous and not possibly of apostolic origin.

**11. 1Co 14 (silence) does not contradict 1Co 11a (prophesy).**

**A.** It is a fact that nothing in 1Co 11a (prayer and prophecy) specifically states that the setting is a church meeting. To conclude such is an assumption.

**B.** The greater context leading up to 1Co 11a concerns the eating of food at private dinner engagements, not church meetings.

　1. This private setting runs all the way back to 1Co 8 (food sacrificed to idols). The desired application there is, "Be careful, however, that the exercise of your freedom does not become a stumbling block to the weak" (11:9).

　2. 1Co 9 (the right of an apostle to full time support) is written as an example of the extent to which Paul was willing to go to not to be a stumbling block. Thus, "we did not use this right. On the contrary, we put up with anything rather than hinder the gospel of Christ" (9:12B), and "I make myself a slave to everyone, to win as many as possible" (9:19), and "I do all this for the sake of the gospel" (9:23).

　3. Accordingly, 1Co 10 goes back to the main subject of meat sacrificed to idols (and not presenting a stumbling block). Paul begins with a warning from Israel's history, "these things occurred as examples to keep us from setting our hearts on evil things as they did" (10:14). Next, to buttress his argument, he appeals to the Lord's Supper, "flee from idolatry . . . You cannot have a part in the both the Lord's table and the table of demons" (10:16, 21). Then, in conclusion of the sacrificial meat issue, he appeals, "whatever you eat or drink or what you do, do it all for the glory of God. Do not cause anyone to stumble . . ." (10:31-32).

　4. Thus, there is no evidence that Paul just suddenly and without introduction began writing about church meetings in 1Co 11. Therefore, 1Co 11a is likely also dealing with activities that would occur in a private setting, apart from the assembled church, as when Deborah went to Barak with a personal word from the Lord (Jdg 4), Huldah had a private audience with the King's representatives (2Ki 22), or Anna spoke specifically to the parents of Jesus among the bustle at the temple courts (Lk 2). Since 99% of one's prayer life occurs *outside* of a church meeting anyhow, this makes perfect sense.

**C.** The actual instructions for church meetings apparently do not begin until 11:17, "In the following directives I have no praise for you, for your meetings do more harm that good. In the first place, I hear that when you come together as a church . . ." Such statements imply that the previous information was about prayer and prophecy uttered apart from a church meeting.

**D.** 1Co 14 clearly refers to a church meeting and teaches the silence of women. In 1Co 11a (prayer and prophecy), it is nowhere specifically stated that the setting is a church meeting. Letting the clear interpret the unclear, the logical conclusion is to understand the prayer and prophecy of 1Co 11a to occur informally, outside the meeting, at a time when women can speak.

**E.** It is a fact that Paul had been in Corinth before writing this letter to them. Indeed, he established the church there! Paul had already taught the church, in person, something about women speaking. Thus, before they ever read Paul's letter to them, the Corinthians were aware of Paul's beliefs regarding women speaking in church (whatever those beliefs were). Supposing that the women were already silent, per Paul's previous instructions, then when 1Co 11 (about prayer and prophecy) was read, the readers would have automatically understood that Paul had in view occurrences of informal prayer and prophecy, not 1Co 14 church meetings.

**F.** The use of the word "churches" in 11:16 does not necessarily refer to church meetings per se, but rather to the totality of Christians living in various geographic locations. The idea is that just as none of the "churches" would have condoned adultery (a sin that obviously would not occur in the actual assembly), neither did the churches have any other practice regarding head coverings.

**G.** One of the reasons given for head coverings is simply, "because of the angels" (11:10). Angels can be present at church meetings, but they can also tune in to private gatherings where prayer and prophecy occur. Hopefully, much more prophetic and prayerful activity goes on during the week than during the few hours of a Sunday church meeting. And, if the intended head covering is long hair (11:15), a woman would be covered twenty-four hours per day, seven days a week, precisely those time when she would pray and prophesy.

**H.** According to Gordon Fee, "It was traditional for exegetes, especially in some Protestant traditions, to argue that women did not really pray and prophesy, but that Paul's language had to do only with their being present in divine services when prayer and prophecy were going on, or to their private praying" (*NIC on First Corinthians*, p. 497, footnote #22).

**12. No long explanation was needed.** Hellenistic culture just happened to be consistent with God's order at this point. **First**, in Jewish synagogues women were not allowed to speak publicly, and many of the early believers came from such a background. **Second**, the Greek biographer, Plutarch, wrote that the voice of modest women ought to be kept from the public, and that they should feel as much shame over being heard as over being stripped (Reinecker, *Linguistic Key*, 438). **Third,** throughout the pagan world, women were (quite wrongly) generally regarded as inferior to men (Guthrie, *New Testament Theology,* 774). **Fourth,** it is a fact that women were not allowed to speak at all in the gatherings of the secular Greek city-state *ekklesia* (Piper and Gruden, *Recovering Biblical Manhood and Womanhood,* p.153). This accounts for why no lengthy explanations were necessary to support these instructions. And as has been previously observed, the women were already silent in the church meetings. This was not a new practice.

Given this historical context, if Paul had actually intended for women to be allowed to speak in church, he probably would have had to write extensively to convince his readers of such an abnormal practice. However, no such argument can be found in the NT. Instead, there is the command for silence; a command not based on the culture of Paul's day, but upon the universal practice of all the churches, upon the tenor of the Hebrew Scriptures (the "Law," v 34), and upon the "Lord's command" (14:37). Contrary to his culture, Paul certainly did assert the equality of the sexes (Ga 3:28), but he still maintained the God-ordained subordination of wives to their husbands (1Co 11, 1Co 14, Ep 5:22ff, Col 3:18, 1 Ti 2:11-13). This family order is to be upheld with the realm of the church meeting also. It is a matter of function and order, not equality.

**13. 1Co 14:33b-35 is not a quotation.** One way some avoid the offense of 1Co 14:33-35 is to make it merely something that really belongs in quotation marks! Under this scheme, the paragraph on women's silence is treated as if it were a quotation from a letter the Corinthians had previously written to Paul (1Co 7:1), with 14:36-38 constituting Paul's shocked response to their absurd idea. This quotation scheme is unlikely for several reasons:

A. Such an approach is, to say the least, highly subjective and speculative. Really it is just wishful thinking!

B. It would be completely different from Paul's other quotations throughout 1Co, which were very short (this one would be long).

C. Paul does not necessarily disagree with the actual quotations he does cite, but merely qualifies them. Here, he would supposedly be completely refuting it.

**14. 1Co 14:33b-35 is in every known Greek MSS.** Gordon Fee has suggested that 1Co 14:33b-35 is a gloss (addition) that should not be in the Bible at all. He suspects it was added later, by some overzealous (and chauvinistic?) scribe. Such additions are certainly possible, but what is the evidence indicating this has occurred? A gloss is usually detected when Greek manuscripts are discovered that omit what others include. This is not the case at all with 1Co 14:33b-35. The paragraph on women's silence is moved to the end of 1Co 14 in a few mss (it seems to fit better there), but it is nevertheless present and accounted for in every known Greek mss (*The Greek New Testament*, UBS, 1975, p 611).

**15. Silence is the Lord's command.** 1Co 14 is not "just" Paul's opinion, but rather it is the "Lord's command" (14:37). Despite the fact that silence is consistent with first century culture, this is not a cultural consideration. Paul was an apostle, a writer of Scripture, outlining what he received from Jesus Himself as a direct command, and it is not up for revision any more than any other biblical command. To say that this isn't binding on believers today is no different from saying that the New Testament commands concerning holiness aren't binding. Jesus said, "whoever has my commands and obeys them, he is the one who loves Me" (Jn 14:21). All who love the Lord will take seriously the things He commands and seek to obey them to the best of their understanding.

Please do not misunderstand. I do not mean to imply that all those who honestly take a different view than mine do not love the Lord! And, one must be careful in this debate to not lose sight of a more fundamental issue. Many brothers (like my associate Dan Trotter) who apply 1Co 14:33b-34 in ways other than I do still hold to a divinely created gender distinction. Dan and I both uphold the value of masculinity and femininity. We both reject the position that homogenizes men and women and transforms them into bland, sexless "persons". We both appreciate role differences in the marriage and the church. We both believe the Scripture teaches these role distinctions. The issue upon which we disagree is the *application* of the Scripture to these role distinctions.

## Conclusion

Sometimes those who "explain away" those passages of Scripture that seem to limit women's roles in ministry fail to see the overall picture of God's family order, set at creation, that encompasses both the

Old Covenant and the New. The church is primarily made up of families. For church order to contradict the order of the family (Ep 5) would be disorder and chaos. The Lord created and gifted men and women with complimentary ministry roles. Truly understanding God's order in both the family and the church causes us to realize that these "limiting passages" are not so much restrictive as protective. They protect women from the burden of leadership and of having to function as men. They also encourage men to be servant leaders. And, He is presenting to us a picture of Christ and His bride, the church, which is submissive to Christ as Head.

The women's silence is both an object lesson and an application of the order that is to exist in the home and the church. It encourages the men to take the lead in the meeting, to be responsible for what goes on, to verbally participate, to begin to articulate their thoughts, to learn to be leaders, etc. For instance, one wife joyously observed that the quieter she was in the interactive church meeting, the more her passive husband spoke up and took the lead (cp 1Pe 3:1-2).

This is a serious issue with far reaching consequences regardless of how it is applied. We all have to do something about this passage at least on a weekly basis, and for me the simplicity of taking God's words at face value is the only approach with which I am at peace. My purpose in writing has been to offer a biblical alternative to the prevailing approaches that are common today, not to attack those who hold views contrary to mine. It has not been convenient for me to hold to the above application and frankly, I sometimes wish I did not see it the way I do. Over the years I have received a storm of contentious protest over my understanding of this passage, wherein both my motives and even ancestry were questioned! According to some I am part of a "devilish scheme" of Scripture "twisting". I thus feel keenly the importance of being careful to respect those who sincerely hold to applications which differ from one's own position. For those reading this who have not made a decision on how to apply 1Co 14:33b-35, please realize that we can not simply stick our heads in the sand and pretend this passage does not exist. As Paul warned, "If he ignore this, he himself will be ignored" (14:38).

— Steve Atkerson

*(For the unabridged version of this article, see "The Lord's Command That Women Remain Silent" at www.ntrf.org)*

VIEW POINT NUMBER TWO

Some have used 1Co 14:34-35 as a basis for silencing women during the gathering of the saints. It is certainly possible to build a case for feminine silence from this passage, and Steve Atkerson has done as good a job as any. However, I believe there are compelling reasons why this conclusion is not warranted from these texts.

Before going further, I think it is useful to reflect a moment on the *interpretive decisions* we all make when we come to Scripture. Why is it that believers reading the same Bible come to very divergent opinions about numerous topics? R.C. Sproul can study Scripture and then write a book titled, *Chosen By God* (Tyndale). Dave Hunt looks at the same Scriptures and pens *What Love Is This?* (Loyal Pub.). His conclusions are diametrically opposed to Sproul's. Norman Geisler tackles the same issues in *Chosen But Free* (Bethany House), and tries to find "a balanced view of divine election." It is obvious that something very mysterious is going on here as people interpret the Bible. If each of you were to read these three books, you would find certain arguments that convinced you, some that confused you, some that made you very upset, some that were new to you, and some that you found very weak. We all claim that we want the Holy Spirit to reveal the truth of Christ, yet we must be aware that there can be sinister forces at work in each of us that keep us, in varying degrees, from discerning the Lord's mind. Even those with the sincerest motives can come to errant conclusions based on limited perspectives and incomplete information. These realities drive us to see again the importance of *humility* as we deal with the Word together with our brothers and sisters. A humble person is truly open to learn, ready to listen to the possible insight of others, and willing to modify his position if the evidence warrants it. What causes me to be persuaded by a line of thought that seems "clear," while you remain unconvinced because it seems "unclear," is a phenomenon not easy to unravel. But we must continue to listen to each other in love and pray that the Spirit will break through our prejudices and darkness with the light of His truth.

With these basic thoughts as a backdrop, I would like to suggest some reasons why the use of 1Co14:34-35 to silence women during the meeting is extremely questionable. First, it would appear that Ac 2:17-18 must have some sort of *hermeneutical priority* in this discussion. In the age of the Messiah the Spirit will cause both males and females to prophesy. Now if Paul desires *prophecy* to be central in the meeting of the saints, what would lead us to believe that only males can prophecy in such a gathering? Wouldn't it be *natural*, and in line with Ac 2:17-

18, for both sexes to participate in prophesying? Peter uttered the fulfillment of Joel 2:28 on the heels of men and women supernaturally speaking in foreign languages. It is claimed, in response, that the Day of Pentecost was not a church meeting. But that is not really true. The 120 disciples, men and women, had been praying in an upper room (Ac 1:13-15). Pentecost occurred in the setting of a body gathering, with fervent prayer being offered by both sexes. *Women were not silent in the upper room, and they were not silent on the day the ekklesia formally began.*

Next, it must be noted that in order for the silence position to stand, *it is required that Paul's epistle be read backwards instead of forwards.* From the flow of Paul's thought in 1Co11:1 to 14:34-35 you would never know that women must be silent during the meeting described in chapter 14. In 1Co 11:2-16 Paul discusses his concern that women pray and prophecy properly. The notion that 1Co 11:2-16 does not assume a meeting of the saints with both sexes present *is very much a minority view.* The great majority of exegetes and commentators – even those who ultimately believe women are to be silent – agree that a "worship service" is in view. In line with Ac 2:17-18, *Paul has no problem with women praying or prophesying in the gathering.* His concern is that it is done *properly.* In the next section, 1Co 11:17-34, obviously it is assumed that women are participating in the Lord's Supper. In chapter 12 the emphasis is that *every saint is gifted and has an important contribution to make to the health of the body.* No exclusion of women from this perspective is given. In chapter 13 Paul shows the centrality of love in our dealings with one another in the body. Women are certainly not excluded or restricted in this regard! Then in chapter 14 he talks about the gathering of the brethren, and he is correcting some matters that were out of balance. In the course of this correction, he seems to assume that the whole body, males and females, are participating: "the person speaking in a tongue…the person prophesying…I wish all of you would speak in tongues…let the one speaking in a tongue…If the whole church [men and women] comes together and all speak in tongues…but if all prophesy…When you come together, each and every one of you has a song, a teaching…you may all prophesy one by one, that all may learn and all may be comforted…" *There is nothing in Paul's line of argument to this point to suggest that only male believers were participating.* It is very *natural* to see the whole body as contributing. In order for the silence position to avoid this clear inclusion by Paul of *all believers,* it must aver that "brothers" in this context means *men* only. Such a response is arbitrary and out of kilter with the apostle's line of reasoning. Reading Paul's epistle *forwards* yields the input of all. Starting with 1Co 14:34-35 and going *backwards* results in the arbitrary silencing of women. To use the concern Paul expresses in 14:34-35 as a means of canceling out the natural flow of thought in the context that seems to include all saints, is a very questionable way of interpreting Scripture. It would seem to be a more probable assumption that the prohibition in 14:34-35 has some other explanation and was not meant to silence the sisters entirely during the meeting.

Further, it would seem to be a very strange situation if women are *allowed to prophesy everywhere but where Paul sees it as mattering most – in the meeting of the saints*. Paul very clearly assigns to prophecy a central place in the saints' meetings. He makes statements like, "the whole church comes together and all prophesy," and yet the silence position asks us to believe that women are excluded from this activity in such a meeting. Wouldn't it be more natural to assume that if men and women are to prophesy in the Messianic age, that they would both do it where it counts most, in a 1Co 14-type gathering? What about Philip's four virgin daughters who prophesied (Ac 21:9)? Are we to believe that these gifted ladies would not prophesy in the context of the gathered saints, where such an activity was to be the center point? Again, it would be *natural* to assume that feminine prophesying took place in the 1Co 14 meeting, which coincides with the information in 1Co 11:2-16. The silence position leads us to the *unnatural* conclusion that female prophesying can only happen *outside* of where Paul sees it as most important, *inside* the body meeting described in 1Co 14.

The silence position militates against the very thing we all are for – *open meetings with mutual participation*. In all the key ways, *about half the priesthood has to be quiet*. It really boils down to a meeting where the males participate. Paul says, on the other hand, "each and every one of you [*hekastos*] has a song, a teaching, etc." (1Co 14:26). This is another perspective that would at least make you wonder if using 14:34-35 to silence sisters is correct. It seems to me that Paul desires for the ladies to participate with their husband's blessing, while in submission to their husbands.

It may help clarify the situation if we consider the general ministry of the Word in the assembly. Christ rules his *ekklesia* by his Word. That Word will have a number of goals – encouragement, comfort, admonition, rebuke – and will come through different channels – singing, teaching, prophesying, various words shared by the brethren. Remember, in the New Testament even singing is part of the teaching and admonishing dimension of our life together (Ep 5:19; Col 3:16). Thus,

Paul has no issue with sisters praying, prophesying and singing, but they are not, according to 1Ti 2:11-12, to publicly teach the assembly. The sisters participate in the broad teaching ministry of the church in many ways, for even when they prophesy, others learn. The ministry of Christ's Word is given to the entire congregation, and it will come to expression in many different ways. In all of this, it does not appear that women are required to be silent.

What, then, is 1Co14:34-35 talking about? I have studied this for years, and the best sense I can make out of it is summarized by Dr. Richard Pratt and R. McLaughlin: "As he began to define this more clearly [in 1Co 14:26], he pronounced a general policy that *everyone* should come to worship ready to use his or her spiritual gifts . . . . Paul's point was that there should be no bystanders in worship. Each person should bring a gift of some kind, whether ordinary (e.g., a hymn) or extraordinary (e.g., a revelation) . . . . Activities in worship must be practiced *for the strengthening of the church* . . . . Paul applied this general principle to three main issues: speaking in tongues (14:27-28); prophecy (14:29-33); and women (14:34-35) . . . . The instruction to *weigh carefully what is said* (14:29) raised a particular issue related to wives. It is likely that here (as in 11:2-16) Paul had in mind wives, not women in general. How should wives honor their husbands who prophesy, and at the same time weigh what their husbands say? . . . It must be remembered that Paul did not believe women should not speak in church at all. In 11:5,13 he explicitly acknowledged their right to pray and prophesy. Rather, they should not ask questions . . . . In this context, he seems specifically to have prohibited wives from questioning their own husbands in church. It seems best to read this passage as returning to the issue of wives honoring their husbands in public worship . . . . it was important for wives not to embarrass their husbands by challenging their prophecies in public ("Love Is Our Guide: 1 Cor.14:1-40," IIIM Magazine Online, 24:4, 2002, pp.8,9; www.thirdmill.org/files/english/new_testament/; another excellent study, "What Did the Apostle Mean By, 'Let Your Women Keep Silence in the Churches,'" by Rusty Entrekin, can be seen at www.thingstocome.org/silence.htm).

A key assumption of the silence position is that 1Co 11:2-16 does not refer to a 1Co 14-type of gathering. Even though most exegetes agree that it does refer to such a meeting, advocates of the silence position hold that the greater context leading up to 1 Cor.11:2-16 concerns the eating of food at private dinner engagements, not church meetings. But this does not appear to be entirely true. In 1Co 10:14-22, Paul specifically mentions the Lord's Supper, "you cannot have a part in both the Lord's Table and the table of demons." Further, 11:2, "I praise you for remembering me in everything and for holding to the teachings, just as I passed them on to you," indicates a transition into another concern Paul is going to deal with. This concern, as Ben Witherington III notes, relates to "praying and prophesying in Christian worship" (*Conflict & Community in Corinth*, Eerdmans, 1995, p.235).

The difficulty of putting things in black-and-white categories can be illustrated when Steve Atkerson suggests that "the silence is limited to speaking." He believes that "women are not to make comments designed for the whole church to hear." But in Ep 5:19 singing is called "*speaking* to one another." So does this mean that women cannot sing in the meeting? Making melody is also said to involve "teaching and admonishing" (Col 3:16). What if the Lord gives a sister a song to sing to the congregation? Is that wrong? Must she teach her husband so he can sing it to the group? We know for a fact that women uttered prayers heard by the 120 in the upper room, and they burst forth with tongues the wonderful works of God on the Day of Pentecost. To suggest that sisters cannot offer spoken prayers, directed to the Lord but heard by the whole church, is an extreme and unwarranted restriction.

Many feel it is significant that from the early church fathers forward, the church has generally held to the silence of women in the church. Of course, in fairness, it should be noted that they also held to the silence of men in the church! They shut down the priesthood of believers and the hierarchy did all the ministry. The early church fathers are hardly a guide for sound teaching. I do not think Steve would also say, "it is noteworthy that the early church fathers practiced infant baptism, the Lord's Supper as a sacrament, and the bishop as supreme." These fathers held to a very unscriptural view of women as persons, so it is hardly fair to cite their silencing of women as something noteworthy (cf. Uta Ranke-Heinemann, *Eunuchs for the Kingdom of Heaven: Women, Sexuality & the Catholic Church*, Penguin, 1990, 360pp). Since these early church fathers were so wrong on many key issues, one might justly reason that their view of women's role in the church could also very well be in error.

Steve suggests that the passages limiting a woman's ministry are meant to "protect women from the burden of leadership and of having to function as men." Since Paul sanctions the praying and prophesying of the sisters in 1Co 11:2-16, I believe it is a mistake to designate these as male functions. Ac 2:17-18, 1Co 11:5 and Ac 21:9 assign the functions of praying and prophesying to women, not just to men. The answer to women not being in leadership is not to keep them silent, but for them to pray and prophesy under the oversight and with the blessing of their husbands. To posit that for a woman to speak words that the whole church hears is to thereby function as a man is without biblical support. Men and women are to speak to one another as servants unto edification.

Since Paul's flow of thought in 1Co 11-14:33 clearly includes women, it would be wiser to view 14:34-35 as not intended to silence women completely. Since prophecy is unambiguously the center point of the 1Co 14 meeting, it would be natural to see women prophesying in that context, and participation by males and females is certainly suggested by Paul's universal language, "everybody is prophesying." Thus the stricter application is unwarranted and unnecessary, given the weighty contextual considerations. A biblical and "loving approach" would allow women to speak in proper ways and to take seriously the concerns that Paul voices. To take the restriction in 14:34-35 and read it back into the previous context is not a sound hermeneutical method. The brethren read the epistle *forwards* not *backwards*. Women were included up to 14:33. Therefore, the stricter application draws a wrong conclusion from a highly questionable use of the text.

Again, we are back to how each of us is persuaded by certain evidence as we make interpretive decisions regarding texts of the Bible. To me, it is clear that women were included in the flow of Paul's thought, and therefore it is letting the unclear interpret the clear to conclude that Paul meant to totally silence women in 14:34-35. I believe the weight of evidence tips the scale toward the proper participation of women, not toward their silence. The truth is you can build apparent cases from texts for both the participation and the silence of the sisters. Given the immediate announcement on the Day of Pentecost that brothers and sisters would prophesy, and given the fact that prophecy is to be central in the 1Co 14 meeting, I believe it is best to err on the side of allowing the sisters to function, rather than trying to resolve the issue by silencing them.

— Jon Zens

*Many issues just touched upon in this chapter are enlarged upon in Jon's article, "And God Gave Heman 14 Sons & 3 Daughters' (1Chr 25:5-6): A Look At Women in the History of Redemption." — Editor*

# THOROUGHLY BIBLICAL CHURCH

What are the irreducible, minimum requirements for a church in order for it to be biblical? It was argued earlier in this book that the practices passed on by the apostles have the force of biblical command, and this is true be they, for instance, concerning people working and providing for themselves and not being idle, or the manner in which churches functioned (such as what they did when they met together). From the New Testament as a whole we can piece together a clear picture of just what this apostolically commanded church practice actually was. I would consequently list the following:

•Believers met as churches on the first day of the week. (And it is instructive to note at this point that this is the only apostolic practice that the early church fathers didn't mess around with and change. And of course the reason for this is that it doesn't in any way touch on the actual nature of what a church is, and therefore didn't affect the wrong teachings and changes to church practice they introduced one way or the other. They therefore left this one thing unchanged and it remained as the apostles had originally established.)

•When churches came together they met in houses.

•When they came together in their houses their corporate worship and sharing together was completely open and spontaneous (1Co 14:26 describes the proceedings as, "each one has"), with no one leading from the front. The early believers didn't have anything that even approximated a church service.

•As part of these proceedings they ate the Lord's Supper as a full meal, indeed as their main meal of the day, commonly referring to it as the love-feast.

•They understood each church to be an extended family unit (the idea of churches being institutions or organizations would have been totally alien to them), and practiced non-hierarchical plural male leadership that had arisen from within the church those elders would subsequently lead. This indigenous eldership (elder, pastor/ shepherd, bishop/ overseer being synonymous terms in the New Testament) sought to lead consensually wherever possible, and was understood to be purely functional, and not in the slightest way positional.

Now that is what the Bible clearly reveals as to how the apostles, who were the recipients of Jesus' full revelation and teachings, established churches to operate and function. But the question before us is: How much of their blueprint could be changed whilst leaving a church as still fundamentally biblical in it's nature and functioning. (I use this phrase because nature and functioning are totally interrelated, being actually different sides of the same coin. As in the rest of life, form follows function - it is just the way things unalterably are! Parents and children, for instance, function together differently than colleagues at the work place, and it's the difference in nature that makes the difference in function so important. A family where parents and children relate together more like workmates than blood relatives would be an example of, not a normal family, but a dysfunctional one. So likewise, churches that function as institutions or organizations, rather than extended families of the Lord's people, are examples of dysfunctional churches and not, biblically speaking, normal ones.) So let us now proceed in earnest to the answering of our question, and see what parts of the apostolic blueprint, if any, are non-essential in maintaining both the nature and functioning of a biblical church. And we'll start with the issue of which day churches ought to meet.

Now as far as nature and function are concerned this is indeed entirely neutral, and the early church fathers realized this and so saw no need to make changes. They saw that you could alter the functioning and nature of churches without reference to the day on which they met and so in that regard left things as apostolic status quo. And, conversely, a biblical church could change the day on which it got together yet remain everything it already was, and continue to practice and function in the same manner in every other respect.

And I would be the first to say that being (nature) and doing (function) church biblically is more important than the day on which you meet in order to so be and do; and would rather be part of a church that was biblical in practice and function but which met on, say, Thursdays or Tuesdays, than one that met on Sundays but which wasn't biblical according to our earlier definition. But here is my question: When the early church fathers themselves chose not to change the day of the gathering of believers, on what basis, and for what possible reason, should we?

Though I say again that I do accept without reservation that a church meeting on a different day of the week to Sunday can be otherwise fully biblical. Further, if it ever became illegal to meet on Sundays, but not Thursday, then I would probably, under such circumstances, be quite happy to make the necessary changes. But outside of such extenuating circumstances, and I shall be back to that thought later, why change the day on which the early church, under the guidance and care of the apostles, met?

And let me also answer at this point the completely legitimate point that in the world of the New Testament, the Jews started a new day in the evening, and this means the first day of the week for them started on Saturday evening. Therefore, if any church met on Saturday evenings specifically for that reason then I would accept it as a biblical thing to do. However, it must still be said that this would seem to be illogical in countries where each day is reckoned to commence in the morning. For most of us the first day of the week is the time period from when we get up on Sunday morning until we go to bed again, so I would still maintain that meeting as churches on Sundays remains the biblical norm as far as we are concerned. So let's move on now to the question of meeting in houses.

That the early church did meet in houses no one with an ounce Bible knowledge is going to deny, and the nature and functioning of the meetings they had when they came together as churches simply meant that there was never any need for them to do otherwise. Numbers in each church were, by definition, supposed to be small, and interactive gatherings with no one leading, and with a meal thrown in to boot, are just perfect for a house setting. After all, what better place could there possibly be? And so once again we see form following function as it always does in the New Testament. (The eventual move from houses into specially sanctified religious buildings was, as with all the other changes we are considering, due to the early church fathers. And it is interesting to note too that this was the final change they made to the apostolic blueprint, and that meeting in houses was actually the original apostolic praxes that survived their reinvention of the Christian church the longest.)

But let us now consider the plight of twenty Eskimos in a village somewhere near the North Pole who have just become Christians, and who therefore want to become a church, but whose largest igloo can only fit 8 people in it. Now if they therefore decided to hire a slightly larger igloo with the express purpose of using it for their gatherings as a church, then assuming they still meet as the Bible describes and don't therefore change the nature of what their gathering together ought to be, then I would see no problem. Indeed, I would rather be part of a biblical church that met outside of homes for their main gathering (assuming though that the other biblical practices were in place) than part of a church that met in homes but which was unbiblical in every other respect. You can maintain the nature and functioning of a church, if you really have to, whilst meeting somewhere other than in a home. Indeed, the church of which I am a part sometimes used to rent a hall for the bit of our gathering together that includes the singing, this being out of love for neighbors having heard their complaints about the noise. But we sit in a circle, just as we would in a home, and what we do in that hall is still completely open with everyone free to spontaneously take part, and without anyone leading from the front. And when we are done we return to one of our houses for the love-feast. But let me underline now what I just said about if you really have to; because we must make sure that we don't let deviations from the biblical norm, permissible only because of extenuating circumstances, actually become the norm. Let me illustrate what I mean by this from what the Bible teaches about baptism.

Biblical baptism, like apostolic tradition for the way a church functions, is a command from the Lord. And although it's actual mode isn't anywhere commanded in the pages of scripture, we know from the way the early church did it (apostolic tradition again) that it was to be done upon conversion, with no time lapse, and in water. (And of course the immersion bit we get from the simple fact that the actual word baptism in English is simply a transliteration of the Greek word *baptizo* which literally means to dip, dunk or immerse.) And many of us would be greatly concerned at any idea that we are free to make changes to this, whether regarding who is to be baptized, the mode of their baptism, or indeed it's timing, and remain painfully aware of how the church at large has massacred it in each of these ways for far too long. So our position would be that, in order to comply with the teaching of the Word of God, a person should be baptized upon profession of faith in Jesus, as soon as possible, and by full immersion in water.

But let us now address an instance of someone coming to the Lord but who is bedridden because of illness. Baptism, as biblically commanded and exampled in the New Testament, is clearly out of the question as far as they are concerned, so would not coming up with some other more appropriate mode be incumbent upon us? And of course we would respond to this in the affirmative! In such a circumstance one would technically be out of step with the teaching of scripture as to the mode of baptism, yet still be in complete harmony with it's intent and spirit. But here is the vital point: Nothing of what I have just said could possibly apply to the conversion of an able bodied person, and the normal mode would have to be employed in order for things to be as the Lord wants. And neither could anyone argue for baptism for someone

110

who hadn't responded to Jesus by faith, because that would attack the very nature of baptism, even though it's external mode might still in accordance with the scripture.

And of course this is what I mean when I say we must not make biblically permitted deviations, necessitated because of extenuating circumstances, become the norm. If the church of which I am a part here in England had access to the size of houses that similar churches have, for instance, in America, then we would not in a million years have even thought of using a hall for part of our gathering together. And if we return for one moment to our postulated brothers and sisters at the North Pole, should it turn out that they do have igloos big enough to fit a good number of people in after all, then what possible need would they have of hiring a large public building-type igloo for their church gatherings? And of course the truth of the matter is that any process of negotiating away any of these factors which together make a church biblical is usually a lead up to attempts at smuggling in alternatives to the other three things I listed:

•Open worship and sharing with no one leading from the front
•The Lord's Supper as a full meal
•Non-hierarchical, plural, male, indigenous leadership

And do let me make it quite clear that with the above three things we are now looking at the completely non-negotiable and irreducibly bare minimum requirements for a church to be said to be biblical. But let me make it clear as well that I do not by this mean that everything has to be in place from the word go, there is often and frequently the need for instruction, development and spiritual growth first. Yet it still remains the case that these things must be at least where a church is headed, it's destination so to speak, even if it has not yet arrived. Of course the Lord's Supper as a full meal ought to be in place from the word go, there is no possible reason for such to not be the case, but eldership will normatively arise later. And it is often the case too that someone might take an initial lead in the corporate weekly gatherings until others learn how to begin to play their part. But the thing to grasp is that it would nevertheless be quite clear where the church was headed in regards to how it functions and does things.

And of course the issue here is that anything that touches on these three things does indeed impact on the very nature of what a church is. Change things here and you cause a church to begin functioning in a way that is not only different from what the New Testament reveals, but completely alien to it and virtually it's opposite. To return to our example of baptism we might say that here we have the equivalent of baptizing an unbeliever. The very nature of the thing is changed and the Lord's intention for it made void, canceled out; indeed, virtually done away with! And it boils down to this: Why would anyone who understands these last three parts of the blueprint want to play around with the first two in any case, unless there were the most pressing extenuating circumstances virtually forcing them into it? I have yet to hear it put better than by my good friend Steve Atkerson: "The question is not so much why we should do things the same way the apostles did, but rather why would we want to do anything differently?"

And I rather think that says it all!

— Beresford Job

# Part II
## CHURCH MINISTRIES

Some churches are ruled by a single man (pastor, pope, or archbishop). Perhaps such churches could be pigeonholed as benign "dictatorships." Other churches are controlled by the ultimate authority of congregational vote. These could be referred to as "democracies." Finally, many churches operate under the guidance of a plurality of elders. It was argued earlier in this book that the ideal is government by the consensus of the whole church. If this really is the case, they why are elders needed in the church?

### THE ADVANTAGE OF HAVING ELDERS

During the Battle of Midway (World War II), a lone American bomber squadron discovered and attacked the Japanese fleet. Tragically, the squadron had become separated from its fighter escort. The attack proved suicidal. All but one of the men were killed. Elders are to the church what the fighters were to the bombers: protection. They also provide direction, teaching, help the church to achieve consensus and to grow into maturity.

Regarding false teachers, the elders must "refute" those who oppose sound doctrine (Tit 1:9), but even this should ultimately follow the check and balance process of Mt 18:15-35 (Christian discipline). Elders must not be guilty of "lording it over those entrusted" to their care, but instead be "examples to the flock" (1Pe 5:3). Having a plurality of elders (all of whom have equal authority) also tends to prevent any modern Diotrophes from arising (3Jn 9-10). However, despite any church's best efforts, we need to realize that "even from your own number men will arise and distort the truth in order to draw away disciples after them. So be on your guard!" (Ac 20:30-31).

Based on such texts as Ac 20:25-31, Tit 1:9, Ep 4:11-13, 1Ti 1:3 & 3:4-5 & 5:17, 6:20, 2Ti 1:13-14, 2:2, 15, 3:16-17 4:2-4, Tit 1:9, 13 & 2:15, Heb 13:17, the function that leaders are to serve in the church becomes clear. Leaders are to guard and protect against false teachers, train other leaders in apostolic tradition, lead by example, guard the truth, beat off wolves, help achieve consensus, etc. In sum, church leaders are men of mature character who oversee, teach, protect, equip, and encourage the church. Every now and then they will need to call on the church to "submit" (Heb 13:17) to their leadership.

Though they were technically apostolic workers, Timothy and Titus clearly functioned as elders until local elders were appointed. Thus, the elders that they appointed could be expected to do the same types of things that the apostolic workers did on the local level (1Ti 1:3, 4:11, 5:17, 6:17, Tit 1:12-13, 2:15, 3:10). From this is it clear that it is proper for elders, in exercising leadership, to authoritatively reprove, speak, teach, and guide. Elders are to "rule well" and "oversee" the churches, taking the initiative in prompting and guarding. As mature believers, their understanding of what constitutes right or wrong behavior and doctrine will most probably be correct. They naturally will often be among the first to detect and deal with problems. However, if those they confront refuse to listen, the elder's only recourse is to then present the matter to the whole church in accordance with the Mt 18 process. Authority, ultimately, still rests with the church corporately.

There is a delicate balance to be reached between the leading role of elders and the ecclesia-type responsibilities of the church as a whole. Too far one way and you set up a pope. Too far the other and you have a ship with no rudder. In essence, both arguments for the leadership of the elders and for the corporate responsibility of the entire church are valid. These need to both be emphasized. On one hand, you have elders leading by example, guiding with teaching and by moderating the give-and-take discussion of the assembly. They have no final right of veto on any of the proceedings. On the other hand, you have the flock. They can do what they want but are exhorted to follow their elders and to allow themselves to be persuaded by their arguments. Elders' words have weight because and only to the extent that the people give it to them. Elders deserve honor due to the position God has placed them in. This idea is similar to the way elders were respected in Israelite towns throughout the Old Testament. They did not have any actual authority or power, but they sure did accord a great deal of respect. To not listen to the wisdom of an elder was tantamount to calling yourself a fool and a rebel.

### ELDER LED CONSENSUS

All are agreed that the Lord Jesus is the head of the church (Col 1:15-20). Thus, the church ultimately is a dictatorship (or theocracy) ruled by Christ through His written word and the influence of the Holy Spirit (Jn 14:25-27; 16:12-15; Ac 2:42; Ep 2:19-22; 1Ti 3:14-15). Once we follow the organizational flow chart down from the head, where does the line of authority go?

In speaking to the "elders" of the Ephesian church (Ac 20:17),

Paul said, "Keep watch over yourselves and all the flock of which the Holy Spirit has made you overseers. Be shepherds of the church of God which He bought with His own blood" (20:28). The presence of the terms "overseers" and "shepherds" certainly suggests a supervisory position for elders. When writing to Timothy about the qualifications for an elder, Paul asked, "If anyone does not know how to manage his own family, how can he take care of God's church?" (1Ti 3:5). This again implies a management role for elders. Peter asked the elders to "be shepherds of God's flock that is under your care, serving as overseers" (1Pe 5:2); once more elders are painted in a leadership mode. 1Ti 5:17 refers to elders who "direct the affairs of the church well." 1Th 5:12 asks the brothers to respect those "who are over you in the Lord and who admonish you." Heb 13:7 commands, "Remember your leaders." Following that, Heb 13:17 reads, "Obey your leaders and submit to their authority. They keep watch over you as men who must give an account." All of this indicates that there are to be human "leaders" in the church. These leaders are most often referred to as "elders" or "overseers." (As to the difference between an elder, overseer ("bishop" in the KJV), and pastor (shepherd), an examination of Ac 20:17, 28-30; Tit 1:5-7; and 1Pe 5:1-3 will show the synonymous usage of the words. All three refer to the same office. Any modern distinction between them is purely artificial and without Scriptural warrant.)

The above references to "rule" by overseers could, if taken in isolation, easily lead to a wrong view of how elder rule should operate. There is more to the equation. Consider the steps of church discipline in Mt 18:15-17 as it relates to a church's decision making process (see also 1Co 5:1-5; Ga 6:1). Notice that the whole congregation seems to be involved in the decision to exercise discipline. Notice also that the leaders are not especially singled out to screen the cases before they reach the open meeting nor to carry out the disciplining. It is a corporate decision.

This corporate process is also glimpsed in Ac 1:15-26. The apostle Peter placed the burden for finding a replacement for Judas upon the church as a whole. In Ac 6:1-6, the apostles turned to "all the disciples" (6:2) and asked them to choose administrators for the church's welfare system. Both these examples point to congregational involvement.

Paul wrote to "all" (1:7) the saints in Rome, and made no special mention of the elders. The letters to the Corinthians were addressed to the entire "church" (1Co 1:2, and 2Co 1:1). Again there was no emphasis on the overseers. The greeting in Ga 1:2 focuses on the "churches" in Galatia. The message was not first filtered through the leaders. The

"Saints in Ephesus" (1:1) were the recipients of that letter. In Php 1:1 the saints were given equal billing with the overseers and deacons. In Col 1:2 the salutation went to "the holy and faithful brothers in Christ." All of this implies that the elders were themselves also sheep. The elders were a subset of the church as a whole. There was no clergy/laity distinction.

This lack of emphasis on the leadership is also seen in 1Th 1:1; 2Th 1:1; Jam 1:1; 1Pe 1:1; 2Pe 1:1; 1 Jn 2:1, 7, and Jude 1:1. In fact, the book of Hebrews was written to a subgroup of believers and it was not until the very last chapter that the author asked them to "greet all your leaders" (13:24). He did not even greet the leaders directly!

In Heb 13:17, believers are encouraged to "obey" church leaders. Interestingly, the Greek behind "obey" is not the regular Greek word for "obey." Instead, *peitho* is used, which literally means "to persuade" or "to convince." Thus, Heb 13:17 should be rendered "let yourselves be persuaded by." This same verse also instructs believers to "submit" to the authority of their church leaders. As with "obey," the common Greek word for "submit" is not used. Instead, *hupeiko* was chosen by the author, a word meaning "to give in, to yield" after a fight. It was used of combatants. The idea behind *hupeiko* is seen in Southern General Robert E. Lee's letter to his troops concerning their surrender at Appomadox: "After four years of arduous service, marked by unsurpassed courage and fortitude, the Army of Northern Virginia has been compelled to yield to overwhelming numbers and resources."

Thus, God's flock is to be open to being "persuaded by" (*peitho*) its shepherds. In the course of on-going discussion and teaching the flock is to be "convinced by" (*peitho*) its leaders. Mindless slave-like obedience is not the relationship pictured in the NT between elders and the church. Of course, there will be those times when some in the flock can't be completely persuaded of something and an impasse will arise. When necessary to break the gridlock , the congregation is to "give in to, to yield to" (*hupeiko*) the wisdom of its leaders.

Much may be gleaned from the way that NT writers made appeals directly to entire churches. They went to great lengths to influence ordinary "rank and file" believers. The apostles did not simply bark orders and issue injunctions (as a military commander might do). Instead, they treated other believers as equals and appealed directly to them as such. No doubt local church leaders led in much the same way. Their primary authority lay in their ability to influence. The respect they were given was honestly earned. It was the opposite of military authority wherein soldiers respect the rank but not necessarily the man.

## Chapter 11:  The Ministry of Elders

Heb 13:7 reflects the fact that the leadership "style" employed by church leaders is primarily one of direction by example: "Remember your leaders . . . Consider the outcome of their way of life and imitate their faith." Along this same line, 1 Th 5:12-13 reveals that leaders are to be respected, not because of automatically inferred authority of rank, but because of the value of their service – "Hold them in highest regard in love because of their work." Jesus said, "You know that the rulers of the Gentiles lord it over them, and their high officials exercise authority over them. Not so with you. Instead, whoever wants to become great among you must be your servant, and whoever wants to be first must be your slave" (Mt 20:25-28).

As pointed out in a previous chapter, the word "church" in the NT is used to refer to the universal church, city-wide churches, and house churches. No organized church is any bigger than a single city, and has no official jurisdiction or authority over any other church (though there naturally will be inter-church cooperation and assistance). Each church is ideally to be guided by a plurality of leaders. Each elder is equal in authority to all the other elders (there is no "senior" pastor). Their primary authority is based on their ability to persuade with the truth. They are to lead by example, not "lording it over" the church. Church polity is thus a dynamic process of interaction, persuasion, and right timing between the shepherds and the sheep.

### THE APPOINTMENT OF ELDERS

How should elders be appointed? Paul required all potential overseers to be able to meet a lengthy list of requirements (1Ti 3:1-7; Tit 1:5-9). That a man is willing and able to be an elder is obviously the work of the Holy Spirit (Ac 20:28). Once these prerequisites are met, the would-be elder is then appointed. In Ac 14:23 Paul and Barnabas apparently did the appointing, and Titus was left in Crete by Paul to appoint elders (Tit 1:5). As Nee observed, "they merely established as elders those whom the Holy Spirit had already made overseers in the church" (*The Normal Christian Church Life*, 41). After the apostles (missionaries/church planters) appointed elders and moved on, there is virtual silence as to how subsequent elders were or ought to be chosen. Operating from the principle of Ac 1:15-26 & 6:1-6, one could be led to conclude that the succeeding elders were chosen by the whole congregation (following the requirements laid out in 1Ti 3:1-7), under the leadership of the existing elders, and under the advisement of any apostles that have earned the right to be heard by that local congregation.

## THE PRESBYTERY

Is there supposed to be one elder per church, several elders per church, or several churches per elder? In Ac 14:23, Paul and Barnabas "appointed elders in each church". The biblical evidence seems to support a plurality of elders in every church. However, a bit of confusion arises over the NT pattern of having a plurality of elders per church. From the NT perspective there is technically only one church per city! For instance, Ac 8:1 mentions "the church at Jerusalem," Paul wrote to "the church of God in Corinth" (1Co 1:2) and to "the church of the Thessalonians" (1Th 1:1). Jesus told John to write to "the" church of God in Corinth (1Co 1:2) and to "the" church in Ephesus, "the" church in Smyrna, "the" church in Pergamum, etc. (Re 2:1, 8, 12, 18; 3:1, 7, 14). Thus, Scripturally speaking, there is but one church in Atlanta, one in London, one in Moscow, etc.

In *The Normal Christian Church Life*, Watchman Nee observed, "in the Word of God we see no church that extends beyond the area of a city" (48). When referring to large geographical areas, the Bible uses the word "church" in the plural. For example, "He went through Syria and Cilia, strengthening the churches" (Ac 15:41), "the churches in the provinces of Asia" (1Co 16:19), "the Macedonian churches" (1Co 8:1), "the churches of Galatia" (Ga 1:1), "the churches of Judea" (Ga 1:22), etc. Thus, there is no such thing in the NT as a national church, or a regional church. The only reason for division among churches is geographic location. Mention is made, of course, of the universal church (Ep 1:22-23; 3:10, 21; 5:23-32; Col 1:18) to which all believers of all time belong, but the universal church is invisible and spiritual, with no universal earthly organization. An examination of the NT will reveal that, though all churches were united under Christ as head, there was no outward ecclesiastical organization uniting them. Though cooperating voluntarily together, each church was autonomous. Theirs was a strong inward bond, a spiritual oneness of life in the Lord. Though independent of outward government, they were interdependent in responsibility to one another (see 2Co 8-9).

Then, as a subset of the one city-wide church, there were numerous churches that met in various homes within each city (Ro 16:5; 1Co 16:19; Phm 2; Col 4:15). The relationship between the various house churches is similar to the relationship between the various city churches: all are united under Christ as Head, but there is to be no outward ecclesiastical organization uniting them. All are to cooperate together in interdependence, yet each remain autonomous.

So, did the plurality of elders lead the city-wide church as a whole, or only individual house churches? That elders worked together is clear from Php 1:1, 1Ti 4:14 & Tit 1:5, but it would be a mistake to conclude that they collectively were "over" multiple churches as some sort of ruling presbytery. Since any elder's authority lies solely in his ability to persuade with the truth, and since any respect due him is earned is via personal interaction, there is no way a presbytery of elders could minister "over" a group of churches anyhow. Ideally, each house church should have its own elders. In those transitional situations where a house church has no one qualified to be an elder, temporary leadership could be sought from a respected apostle, an elder in a nearby church, or itinerant pastor-teacher. The NT pattern is for each house church to led by a body of equal brothers (some of whom are elders) leading the church, depending upon one another, accountable to one another, submitting to one another, and living out a mutuality in ministry.

CONCLUSION

Harvey Bluedorn wrote an excellent summary of the ministry of elders, which he entitled, "A Statement on Biblical Eldership and Authority in The Assembly."

**1. The New Testament Standard** — As the pattern of things shown to Moses established the standards for the tabernacle [Ex 25:9,40; 26:30; 39:42,43; Ac 7:44; Heb 8:5], and as the pattern of things shown to David established the standards for the temple [1Ch 28:11-13,19], so the pattern of things shown in the New Testament establishes the standards for the assembly, the temple of God [1Co 3:9,16,17; 6:19,20; 2Co 6:16; Ep 2:21,22; 4:13-16; 1Ti 3:15; 1Pe 2:5,9; Re 1:6; 3:12; 5:10; 20:6].

**2. Servant Leaders** — Leaders are a functional necessity for the assembly. The Lord Jesus raises up men from among the members of the body, and equips them to meet stated qualifications. They will inevitably emerge from among the membership and become apparent to the assembly, and the assembly must formally recognize the Lord's calling in those whom the Lord has truly gifted and qualified to serve as guides, teachers, and examples to the whole body. Such servants are called elders and overseers, or shepherds and teachers [Tit 1:5; Ep 4:11].

**3. Multiple Elders** — A plural number of elders will ordinarily emerge from the membership of an assembly [Acts 14:23], although in a newly formed assembly it may require some time to pass before the Lord fully equips and qualifies elders [Lk12:42; 1Co 4:2; 1Ti 3:6,10; 5:22; Tit 1:5; Heb 5:12,13].  Among the pastor-elders there are some who especially toil in discourse and teaching [Ep 4:11; 1Th 5:12,13; 1Ti 5:17].

**4. Decisions by Full Agreement** — Decisions are made by the full agreement of the assembly, as represented in the men of the assembly, under the advise and counsel of their servants, the elders. Presumably, the men may, by full agreement, delegate certain on-the-spot-type decisions to someone, including to elders, but they must always reserve the right to make the decision themselves, or to determine the policy for such decisions, and they must require of those to whom they delegate decisions a full report and accountability to the assembly.

**5. Elders are Servants, Not Lords** — The Word of Christ rules by His Spirit in the midst of His people, through the regenerate hearts and renewed minds of the members of the assembly as He brings them to complete mutual agreement, unanimous accord, or consensus.  Elders lead by the moral authority of a servant who provides word and example, and who commands respect for what he gives, not for what he requires. Elders do not rule as independent authorities. Their role is advisory and supervisory, not the lordly authority of command and conform.  Elders are instrumental, through their leadership, teaching, and example, in bringing about consensus in the assembly, but all authority rests in Christ alone. All members - including elders - submit to the Lord, then to one another in the Lord - including elder members, who submit to other members, including to other elder members.  In other words, there is no chain of command - God, then Christ, then elders, then members - but only a network of submission, and elders have the greatest burden of submission and accountability because they are servants to the whole assembly.  Only those who humble themselves to the level of servants before the Lord and His assembly may be raised to this level of accountability.  By the nature of the case, those who would exalt themselves to a position of authority over all, have necessarily disqualified themselves from a position of service.

**6. The Saints are Kings and Priests** — It is a severe violation of the adult conscience to treat the saints as children under the overlordship of elders.  The ultimate effect of treating the saints as children is that they will either remain children in their understanding as they submit to bondage, or they will rebel.  Elders exercise appropriate authority as fathers within their own households, but their role in the assembly is not as fathers and lords over children and servants, but as elder brothers in the faith and humble servants to the whole.

**7. A Deliberative Assembly** — The gathered assembly is a deliberative body. The men (adult males) in the assembly are encouraged to interact in an orderly manner with the reading, exhortation, and teaching in the assembly, regardless of what form that interaction assumes - informative lecture, thoughtful consideration and discussion of propositions of Scripture, logical debate of different sides of a question, or consultation on practical issues. This is not a "Quaker-like" meeting of "whenever-the-spirit-leads," nor is it a "family-friendly-style" meeting of token affirmations by heads of household, nor is it a "worship-centered" meeting of lively entertainment, but it is a genuine discipleship learning process which edifies and brings the whole assembly to maturity in Christ through the interaction of the men of the assembly.

**8. Independent Congregational Accountability** — Each congregation constitutes its own communion and is independently accountable to the Lord, but all true congregations exist within the same spiritual kingdom, they depend upon the same Lord, and they cooperate as much as circumstances require and allow, both on the level of individual persons and on a congregational level. There should be no ungodly jealousy between brother believers, nor between sister assemblies."

— Steve Atkerson

# 12

# WHAT IS A MINISTER?

I have been pointedly wrestling with issues related to Christ's church since 1972. Some matters have crystallized in my thinking, and I would like to share them with you in hopes that meaningful dialogue and serious searching of the Scriptures might take place. We have nothing to fear by looking at the Scriptures together.

The key burden on my heart that I would like to express and develop is this: the ministry of the church as a whole will continue to be crippled as long as we perpetuate the separation of "the minister" from the New Testament vision of eldership, and as long as we functionally divide God's people into "ordained" (clergy) and "uncalled" (laity).

## ELDERS INSTEAD OF "MINISTERS"

The New Testament knows only of "saints, bishops and deacons" (Php 1:1). "Bishops," "pastors" and "elders" all refer to the same body of men (Ac 20:17, 28). The oversight of the church is conceived of as a body of elders (1Ti5:17; Jam 5:14). However, the traditional practice of "calling a pastor" separates this "office" from eldership at virtually every point. Under the New Testament pattern, *laos* (people) and *kleron* (clergy, inheritance) refer to *all* of God's people; hence, elders and deacons are part of the "laity/clergy," not separate from or above it. "Most denominational churches have departed from this pattern by distinguishing between the pastor and the elders. Common practice makes the pastor a full-time employee of the church, while the elders are laymen who function much like a board of directors" (James Stahr, *Interest*, April, 1984, p. 2).

In the traditional Protestant pattern, the pastor has a "call" that the other elders do not possess, the pastor is trained differently than the elders, the pastor is ordained in a different way than elders, the pastor comes from outside the body whereas the elders come from within the body, the pastor can be led to another church whereas the elders are resident, the pastor can have "Rev" next to his name but not so elders, the pastor is paid to carry out various duties (but not the elders), texts that apply to a *body* of elders are applied to "the minister"only, the pastor can occupy the pulpit while the elders rarely (if ever) can, and the pastor determines the direction of the worship service. Interestingly, the traditional Protestant way of doing things actually paralles a non-gospel religious model (with priests and witch doctors) more than it does the simple NT pattern.

## THE SHIFT FROM ELDERSHIP/MUTUAL MINISTRY TO "THE MINISTRY"

No matter what area of church truth I study, it seems that the ultimate source of the problem somehow works itself back to the isolation of "the pastor" from the eldership. The frustrating thing to me is this: even though the best scholarship in Bible study and church history is united in the basic conclusion that "ethical guidance for people recently converted to Christianity . . . was offered at first by a polyform ministry of grace, reflected in the New Testament; but as time went by moral authority was increasingly focused in an ordered ministry of bishops and deacons," those who take this perspective seriously are labeled as "off the wall," "unsound," and "dangerous" (the quotation is from G.W. Forell, *History of Christian Ethics*, Vol.1, 1979, p.39; cf. "One God, One Bishop: The Politics of Monotheism," *The Gnostic Gospels*, Elaine Pagels, 1981, pp.33-56). Given the fact that in the New Testament we are confronted with a "polyform ministry of grace," must we not ask ourselves if the decided shift to the focus on "the ministry" (clergy), which occurred quickly in post-apostolic times, was valid or invalid? Judging by our *practice* we give more credence to the post-apostolic tradition than we do to the direct apostolic teaching (cf. Judy Schindler, "The Rise of One Bishop Rule in the Early Church," *ST*, Summer, 1981, pp. 3-9),

## WILL THE REAL "CLERGY" PLEASE STAND UP?

If we take the New Testament seriously, anything that promotes the traditional "clergy/laity" categories must be stopped. Are those in "the pastorate" willing to renounce the title "Reverend" next to their name (cf. David Foster, "Call No Man Teacher, Father, Rabbi....Or Pastor?," *Journal of Pastoral Care*, Jay Adams, ed.)? The whole mystique that surrounds "the pastor" must be brought into line with Christ's statement to the *apostles*: "you are all brethren." Making unbiblical distinctions among ourselves results in some awful traditions, as the following illustration shows: "It was doubtless with assurance born of the reverence with which he was customarily regarded, that by stamping upon the meeting-house doorway floor [John] Smalley made known to his congregation the moment of his arrival, so that members of importance might rise and make him their obeisance as he passed down the center aisle on Sabbath morning" (Mary L. Gambrell, *Ministerial*

*Training in 18th Century New England*, pp.113-114). We may not duplicate this particular obeisance, but the spirit of this illustration is still repeated a thousand different ways in our day.

### PREACHING: IN THE STREET OR IN THE "SANCTUARY"?

Attached to the institution of "the pastor" is the central duty of preaching. H.M. Carson states that preaching "is the main means by which the people of God are built up in the faith" (*Hallelujah! Christian Worship*, p.72). But it appears that "preaching" in the New Testament is primarily an activity that took place *outside* church meetings (cf. Stuart Olyott, "What Is Evangelism?," *Banner of Truth*, July/August, 1969, pp.1ff.; C.E. Dawson, "The Evangelicals," *Gospel Tidings*, Sept., 1982, p.247). The church must be devoted to apostolic teaching. The elders may often provide the backbone of such instruction in the assembly. But to equate the reign of Christ's word in the church with the pulpit ministry of "the pastor" cannot be substantiated from the New Testament. It would wonderful for those with preaching gifts to exercise them "outdoors," as did George Whitefield. It needs to be remembered that the whole rationale for the "centrality of preaching" is suspect: it arose in a state-church where church attendance was compulsory.

### "THE BODY IS NOT ONE MEMBER, BUT MANY"

One of the most damaging spin-offs that comes with separating "the pastor" from the eldership is the *neglect of the total body*. When it is posited that "the whole weight of the order, rule, and edification of the church" rests on "the pastor," as the Puritan John Owen suggested, there is no way that proper attention can be given to the "whole body" perspective in Ephesians 4:16. J.I. Packer freely admits that the Puritan discussion of gifts "was dominated by their interest in the ordained ministry . . . and questions about other gifts to other persons were rarely raised" ("The Puritans and Spiritual Gifts," *1967 Westminster Papers*, p.15).

### WHERE'S THE NEXT MINISTER'S CONFERENCE?

"The ministry" as separated from the eldership also puts incredible pressure on gifted people that they were never meant to bear. Articles from *Christianity Today* illustrate the obvious: "How Many Hats Does Your Pastor Wear?," "Clergy Divorce Spills Over Into the Aisles," "Who Counsels Ministers When *They* Have Problems?" Since pastors are always "giving out," and because local churches are unable and

unequipped to minister to them, they must go away periodically to con-
ferences attended by those in the same syndrome. Because the New
Testament knows nothing of a "pastoral office" as traditionally conceived, it is no wonder that those in it experience "burn-out" in trying to
measure up to its expectations. Life-fracturing issues like nervous break-
downs, suicide, divorce, incredible family stress, and sexual infidelity
are especially high among the clergy. A recent *Focus On the Family*
intensive survey indicated that 1800 pastors leave the ministry *per month*
in our country among all denominations. When are we going to wake
up and realize that there is something rotten in the state of Denmark?

## MINISTRY: PULPIT OR POLYFORM?

The pastoral institution has probably been the most formative fac-
tor in the shape that church services take (cf. Hezekiah Harvey, *The
Pastor*, 1879 [Backus Books, 1982], pp.27-28). The earliest assemblies knew nothing of a "pulpit," and yet it has become an article of
furniture you dare not question. It is a parallel situation to many who
just assume that the apostles gave "altar calls" in the first century. *Scholarship from all traditions* acknowledge that in the New Testament we
are met with *structured informality*. Note these few examples of many
that could be given:

•1Co14:26-36 "provides a glimpse of the early church at worship.
The service apparently contained a mixture of spontaneous flex-
ibility and traditional formality inherited from the synagogue. Congregational participation is suggested by the words" [of 14:26]
(William Baird, *1 Cor./2 Cor.*, 1980, p.59).
•"In Paul's day the worship service probably was more open than
are today's services" (Leonard J. Coppes, *Are Five Points Enough?*,
p.182)
•"The glimpses we have of worshipping congregations in the New
Testament are of active participants" (Herbert Carson, *Hallelujah!*,
p.29).

Urgent questions arise: in light of our confession that the NT is to
guide us, why are our meetings entirely different than those revealed in
Scripture? Is it right for us to eliminate participation in order to maintain the "centrality of preaching"? Why were such meetings edifying
and good for the early church, but "dangerous" for us? Is the Spirit
informing us in the NT, or do we posit that this inspired information is
no longer relevant?

One argument often ushered forth is that 1Co14 is "early revelation" and is modified by "later revelation." But this is specious reason-

ing on several accounts. First, what is there in the "later" revelation that *contradicts* 1Co14? Second, Hebrews is "later revelation," yet it contains the same emphasis found in Corinthians: "exhort one another daily . . . . do not forsake your assembling . . . but encourage one another." Third, James is "later," yet some commentators see 1:19 as a reference "to the free and unstructured worship of early Christian assemblies" (Curtis Vaughn, *James: A Study Guide*, p.35; cf. Earl Kelly, *James: A Primer for Christian Living*, p.69).

If we are honest, we must confess that the pulpit-tradition is a huge obstacle that blocks obedience to the one-another, participatory dimension of body-life found in the New Testament. David Thomas (in 1898!) summarized the situation well: "The Christian church in assembly, on the same occasion, might have several speakers to address them . . . . If this be so: 1. Should Christian teaching be regarded as a *profession*? It is now: men are brought up in it, trained for it, and live by it, as architects, lawyers, doctors . . . . 2. Is the Christian church justified in confining its attention to the *ministry of one man?* In most modern congregations there are some Christian men who, by natural ability, by experimental knowledge and inspiration, are far more qualified to instruct and comfort the people than their professional and stated minister. Surely official preaching has no authority, either in Scripture, reason, or experience, and it must come to an end sooner or later. Every Christian man should be a preacher. Were the half-hour allotted in church services for the sermon to be occupied by three or four Christly men . . . with the capability of expression withal, it would not only be far more interesting, but more profitably spent than now ("1 Corinthians," *The Pulpit Commentary*, p.459).

## But What About My Paycheck?

People in the ministry can feel threatened by the implications of New Testament eldership. The traditional rationale for supporting a pastor is without Scriptural warrant, and is based on misinterpreted texts. But 1Ti5:17-18 indicates that a congregation is free to help any of its elders, as it is able. As with all the other points connected to "the pastorate," support needs to be put in the context of a body of elders, not in connection with an imagined "pastoral office" (cf. Ronald Hock, *The Social Context of Paul's Ministry: Tentmaking & Apostleship*, Fortress, 1980). Financial help is not to be a motive in elders serving the flock; the assembly is free to help elders; elders are free to work with their own hands (1Pe.5:2; 1Ti.5:17; Ac 20:34-35).

## WHERE'S THE BEEF?

If "the pastor" is such an important cog in church ministry, then why is it so hard to validate such a function in the New Testament? John H. Yoder pointedly summarizes the data: "The most striking conclusion to be drawn from this enumeration is the absence of two offices which are most characteristic of modern Christianity: the 'pastor,' in the sense of one professional minister leading a congregation, and the 'bishop,' in the sense of a minister with authority over several congregations. Both of these terms were originally interchangeable with that of 'elder,' referring to one of several men who shared the leadership in a local council. Henri d'Espines, professor of Calvin's own Geneva University, drew the same conclusion, and has dared to say that Calvin's view of the pastoral office is un-biblical, that 'this state of affairs is deplorable,' and that 'the restoration of the collective pastorate, exercised by a veritable council of elders, is one of the primary conditions of the spiritual renewal which our churches need.' Once again, we see Reformed Biblicism at its best coming out in favor of the authority of the Scripture over the church" ("Biblicism and the Church," *Concern #2*, 1955, p.45).

## ARE YOU SEEING SOME LIGHT?

If you are or have in the past been in the "clergy" role, and you are coming to the conviction that this position originates from unscriptural traditions, there are some practical steps that must be taken on your part.

•Stop using "Reverend" and other religious titles in connection with your name (and encourage those around you to cease using language that assumes the "clergy/laity" distinction).

•Renounce your "clergy" status and see yourself as part of the "laos" of God who has manifestations of the Spirit, along with everybody else, for the good of the body (1 Cor.12:7).

•Teach the body that your "clergy" role and all the expectations that go with it are based on human traditions and not the Gospel.

•Instruct the brethren that all aspects of caring for one another rest with the body, not on some spiritual elite.

•Take concrete steps to de-centralize the function of your gifts in the body.

•Begin a new methodology of truth-seeking and truth-speaking. Instead of "clergy" spoon-feeding the "laity," study important issues *together* from the Word with a view toward finding Christ's will and acting upon it.

•Adopt a teaching style where dialogue occurs and questions/insights from others are encouraged.

•As the body makes concrete changes in the way "church" is done, the emphasis shifts from dependency on one person to edifying multiple participation.

•Your financial support as a clergyperson is admittedly a difficult issue, but needs to be Scripturally and creatively evaluated. Regardless of all the specific circumstances in your case, if it will help the assembly develop its one-another ministries, you at least need to be *willing* to follow Paul's example: "You yourselves know that these hands [by tentmaking] ministered to my own needs and those of others with me. In everything I have pointed out to you that, by working in this way diligently, we ought to support the weak" (Ac 20:33-35). As ministry becomes increasingly shared in the body, it takes the load off one person and frees the congregation to evaluate how its financial resources can be maximized for edification and meeting people's needs.

The "clergy" system is a mammoth institution. Its tentacles reach deep into the inner workings of almost every religious group. Not every "clergy" person takes the New Testament seriously, but those who do need to lead the way by personal example to a paradigm shift which better reflects Christ-centered assembly life. People who withdraw from the traditional "clergy" model out of faithfulness to Christ will usually have a heavy price to pay, but the spiritual rewards are beyond description. The truth is, remaining in a system that has crushed and ruined many people's lives is the wrong price to pay. Why do you suppose 1800 people a month are leaving "the ministry"?

## "We Believe the Bible Is Our Infallible Rule of Faith and Practice"

Many churches make this confession, but do they really take the New Testament seriously enough to evaluate all of their practices in light of it? Such a confession becomes very hollow if it is not backed up by honest hermeneutics and sincere obedience. I'm tired of hearing preachers yell, "If we can't find it in the Bible, we won't believe it or do it." Scripture will not support a host of things that go on unquestioned in churches, yet pastors and those in the pew will become livid if their sacred cows are challenged.

I am submitting my understanding of Scripture to the body of Christ. If you believe I am mistaken, please sharpen me with Scripture. On the other hand, if I have articulated things that are worthy of further reflection, then please follow through on the implications. Are you willing either to come up with the goods (from Scripture) to justify the status quo, or change your thinking and practice in light of the Word?

Below are some books that have helped me in the areas discussed above.

•Campenhausen, Hans von. *Ecclesiastical Authority & Spiritual Power in the Church of the First Three Centuries*, Stanford Univ. Press, 1969.
•Davies, J.G. *The Early Christian Church*, Baker, 1981.
•Goppelt, Leonhard. *Apostolic & Post-Apostolic Times*, Baker, 1980.
•Grudem, Wayne. *The Gift of Prophecy in 1 Corinthians*. Univ Press of America, 1982.
•Hanson, Anthony. *The Pioneer Ministry: The Relation of Church & Ministry*. Westminster, 1961.
•Lindsay, Thomas M. *The Church & the Ministry in the Early Centuries*. James Family Pub., 1977.
•Niebuhr, H. Richard. *The Ministry in Historical Perspectives*, Harper & Row, 1983.
•Warkentin, Marjorie. *Ordination: A Biblical-Historical View*. Eerdmans, 1982.

— Jon Zens

# 13

# *Full Time Ministries*

Famous are the words of Jesus, "It is more blessed to give than to receive." Not so familiar is the context in which this truth was recorded. Jesus' words are not found in any of the four Gospels. These words of Jesus were quoted by the apostle Paul while speaking at a pastor's conference (Ac 20:32-35). Amazingly, Paul was instructing pastors to be in the position of *giving* silver, gold and clothing to the church, rather than receiving such from it!

## ACTS 20

In light of what Jesus said, should pastors earn their living from the church? In Ac 20, Paul gave the Ephesian elders specific instructions on their duty as elders. Concerning finances, Paul stated that he had coveted no one's silver or gold and that he had, in fact, paid his own way by "working hard" (20:34-35) with his hands (compare 18:1ff). Following Paul's example, the elders were also to earn their living from a secular job so as to be able to help the weak and live out the words of the Lord Jesus that it is more blessed to give than to receive. Thus, from Ac 20:32-35 it is clear that elders are generally to be in the financial position of giving to the church, not receiving from it.

## 1 CORINTHIANS 9

But what of 1 Co 9:14 where it is stated that those who proclaim the gospel should "receive their living from the gospel"? We can observe from 1Co 9 that at least three groups made their livings from their ministries during NT times: apostles (9:1-6), the Lord's brothers (9:5) and evangelists (9:14).

According to Paul, various factors combined to justify this truth:
1. A "human point of view" (soldier, vineyard keeper, shepherd).
2. The "Law of Moses" (oxen, temple priests).
3. Spiritual principle/logic (spiritual seed/material harvest), 9:11.
4. The words of Jesus, 9:14.

From a merely "human point of view" (9:8) Paul asked: "Who serves as a soldier at his own expense? Who plants a vineyard and does not eat of its grapes? Who tends a flock and does not drink of thte milk?" (9:7). The answer is obvious. All make their livings from their work, and so should apostles/church planters/missionaries.

Then, from the "Law" (9:8), Paul derived the same truth: "Do not muzzle an ox while it is treading out the grain" (9:9). Applied to apostles, Paul asked "Is it about oxen that God is concerned? Surely he says this for us, doesn't he?" (9:9-10). If oxen can eat from what they do, so can apostles! Then in 9:13, Paul brought in the example of OT priests, asking, "Don't you know that those who work in the temple get their food from the temple, and those who serve at the altar share in what is offered on the altar?" (9:13).

Third, this *senus plenior* ("fuller sense") that the Holy Spirit inspired Paul to see in the Law concerning oxen led Paul to derive this spiritual principle: "If we have sown spiritual seed among you, is it too much if we reap a material harvest form you?" (9:11). Paul concluded that this "right of support" should thus be his "all the more" (9:12).

Paul's final line of defense was found in the words of the Lord who "commanded that those who preach the gospel should receive their living from the gospel" (9:14). If it was true for evangelists, it is true of apostles, too.

1Co 9 specifically concerns the rights of an apostle, someone commissioned by either Jesus or the church to travel around evangelizing and establishing churches (the word "missionary" is never used in Scripture; such people were called "apostles" and "evangelists"). As is clear from the text, all such people have the "right" (9:12) to financial support. Is it wrong to apply this passage to elders? Since Paul waived his apostolic "right" to get his "living" from the gospel (9:15, 18), the example he showed the Ephesian elders seems all the more compelling (see also 1Th 2:9; 2Th 3:7-9).

Oddly, after writing convincingly of the right of apostles in 1Co 9, Paul then added, "But I have not used any of these rights. And I am not writing this in the hope that you will do such things for me." (1Co 9:15). Since Paul did not write this in order the hope that the Corinthians would give him support (1Co 9:15), then why did he write this? Amazingly, 1Co 9 is essentially a parenthetical remark! Paul's main topic began in 1Co 8 and concerned not being a stumbling block to others (re: food sacrificed to idols, 8:9). Paul's waver of his "right" to full-time support (1Co 9) illustrated just how far Paul was willing to go to so as not "not hinder the gospel" (9:12b, 15). Then, in 1Co 10, Paul continued on with his main topic, concluding with "Do not cause anyone to stumble, whether Jews, Greeks or the church of God" (1Co 10:31-32). Thus, Paul's objective in writing 1Co 9 was neither to limit nor extend the categories of those who had the "right" to support from the church. It was merely an illustration.  As such, it reveals that Paul had a very liberal approach to supporting church workers ("Is it about oxen that God is concerned?" and "If we have sown spiritual seed among you, is it too much if we reap a material harvest from you?").

It is true that 1Co 9 deals specifically with the rights of an apostle, not an elder.  But, based on the principles expressed in 1Co 9, would it be committing the unpardonable sin for an elder to make his living from the church?  Based on solely on Ac 20, it would seem that pastors (elders) will generally not receive full tme financial support for their ministries.  However, Ac 20 is not the only passage dealing with this subject!  1Co 9 (above) must be factored in, as must 1Ti 5 (below).

### 1 TIMOTHY 5

Temporarily stationed in Ephesus was Timothy, Paul's traveling companion and fellow apostle (1Th 1:1; 2:6), whom Paul left in Ephesus to squelch strange doctrines (1Ti 1:3).  Concerning the same Ephesian elders as in Ac 20, Paul wrote that elders who did a good job a directing the affairs of the church and who worked hard at "preaching and teaching" were worthy of something called "double honor" (1Ti 5:17).  The, using almost the exact same reasoning as in 1Co 9:9, 1Ti 5:18 states, "For the Scripture says, 'Do not muzzle the ox while it is treading out the grain,' and 'The worker deserves his wages.'"  This parallel should not be minimized.  The implications are clear.

But does "honor" mean "pay?"  No.  From the Greek word *time*, it primarily means "respect".  There is a specific Greek word for "pay" (*misthos*) and, significantly, it is used in 1Ti 5:18 (about employees), but not in 1Ti 5:17 (about elders).  *Time* can in certain contexts mean "price," but since a "price" is the quantity of one thing that is demanded in sale for another, it hardly makes sense in this passage (are elders for sale?).  This same word (*time*) is also used immidately following in 1Ti 6:1, "All who are under the yoke of slavery should consider their masters worthy of full respect (*time*)".  Are slaves to "pay" their masters?  One practical application of this "honor" is that an accusation brought against an elder is not to be received unless it is substantiated by more than one witness (1Ti 5:19).  1Ti 5:19 logically follows 5:17-18 if "honor" refers to "respect" (an "accusation" involves dishonor), but follows awkwardly if "honor" refers to "pay."  A good parallel verse is 1Th 5:12-13, wherein the church in Thessalonica was asked to "respect those who work hard among you, who are over you in the Lord and who admonish you.  Hold them in the highest regard in love because of their work."

However, *time* is also used immediately prior to the passage about elders. In 1Ti 5:3 were "honor" is to be given to widows who are really in need (the NIV renders it as "proper recognition"). This occurrence of *time* obviously means granting the widow more than repect! Giving the widow food, helping her with her house and yard work, visiting her, offering her living quarters if needed, and of course even monetary assistance, is the idea. "Honor" was also clearly understood by Jesus to refer to material support in Mk 7:10. The Law of Moses required, "Honor you father and your mother". Unhappy with the religious leaders of Judaism, Jesus said, "But you say that if a man says to his father or mother: 'Whatever help you might otherwise have received by me is Corban' (that is, a gift devoted to God), then you no longer let him do anything for his father or mother. Thus you nullify the word of God by your tradition that you have handed down" (Mk 7:11-13). Thus, it is within the realm of possibility that in some cases "honor" to an elder might include giving him a love offering, an honorarium.

So why did Paul use *time* ("honor") instead of *misthos* ("wages) in 1Ti 5:17? Perhaps because the elder's relationship to the church is not to be as a hireling. Nor is he to "charge" for his services. Jonathan Campbell has wisely stated, "There is a difference between being paid to do a job and being released to do a work." Concerning voluntary giving (an honorarium) versus a salaried position, Dan Trotter has warned, "The widows of 1Ti 5:3-16 weren't earning a salary, they were receiving charity. And "the laborer is worthy of his hire" quote in Lk 10 referred obviously not to disciples receiving a salary or wages, but hospitality (eat and drink what's set before you, etc.). The word "wages" in the OT quotation (1Ti 5:18) is obviously metaphorical (just like the unmuzzled ox eating straw is metaphorical). If you push that metaphor too far, we'll have Christian workers eating straw! Another example of the metaphorical use of "wages" is where Paul wrote to the Corinthians that he had robbed other churches so as not to accept wages from Corinthians. Vines states that the word "wages" in 2Co 11:8 is clearly metaphorical, which it, of course, is. I don't think its anybody's business to complain if a Christian worker (whether apostle, prophet, elder, teacher, or whatever) receives voluntary offerings from anybody for whatever reason. But the minute a salary or wages is paid, the principle of voluntary giving of service to the body is violated, the principle of clergy-less Christianity is violated, the priesthood of all believers is violated, etc. I'm not getting on that train, because its heading over the cliff. The number one stench in the institutional church is money, plain and simple. It is an abomination, a disgrace not only to God, but to the human race. And once we open the door with a hireling clergy, we are finished. In conclusion, if Paul had meant "double wages" in ITi 5:17, why didn't he say "double *misthos*," or "double *opsonion*", two perfectly clear words which mean "wages" and would have conveyed what he meant? And if he meant wages, why didn't the early church follow his example?"

London elder Beresford Job comments, "I think it unlikely that there would be much need for anyone to be a full time elder unless they also had a ministry wider than just to the house church of which they are a part. It is significant that when Paul addresses this issue when he wrote to Timothy he assumes that any elders who might need some kind of support were precisely those engaged in preaching and teaching, which would lead me to believe he is referring to people who were among the evangelists and pastor-teachers who, with apostles and prophets, comprised the fourfold trans-local ministries of Ep 4:11. I therefore conclude that there are men who are called to share themselves out amongst more than one church who won't necessarily have time to do a secular job as well. Assuming they aren't millionaires, or have a business that supports them and which functions pretty much without needing their attention, they are going to have to be funded from elsewhere.

However, the apparent contradiction we seem to have in scripture is that although the laborer is indeed worthy of his hire (such men have bills to pay and families to support too), ministry is nevertheless free of charge and we see nothing whatsoever in the New Testament of salaried positions. Indeed, the idea of churches 'employing' someone is perfectly at odds with the teaching of the New Testament as a whole. So let me put it to you that what we have is that if someone feels called to a ministry which prohibits them the time to earn money from other employment, then they can well trust the Lord to provide their needs. It will, of course, be through the freewill offerings of the Lord's people, but nothing must be done by the one called into full time service to ever procur money or that transgresses scriptural teaching that all ministry is free of charge.

For myself I have been in full-time ministry for 25 years and don't charge money, don't take collections, have never requested that collections be taken on my behalf, have never mentioned expenses incurred, never sent out a prayer letter or made needs known to others in any way. I finance everything I do myself and simply respond to whatever I believe the Lord would have me do, whether it's driving locally to teach or buying plane tickets for myself and my wife and daughter to come over to the States to do various things as invited. And this I do knowing that if I work free of charge then the Lord will provide for myself and my family in answer to prayer. I call it 'living by faith properly' as opposed to 'living by faith - and hints and prayer letters and collections'."

**1 PETER 5**

What did Peter mean in 1Pe 5:2 when he exhorted the elders to shepherd God's flock voluntarily and not "for sordid gain"? "Sordid gain" is from a single Greek word, *aischrokerdos*. *Aischros* means "shame, disgrace" and *kerdos* means "gain, profit, advantages." A related term, *aischrokerdes*, is used in Tit 1:7 where elders are required not to be "fond of sordid gain." 1Ti 3:3 parallels this with a requirement that elders be free from the "love of money." Thus, *aischrokerdes* is a virtual synonym for being "greedy for money." One idea is that of R.C.H. Lenski (*The Interpretation of the Epistles of St. Peter*, 219), who points out that since elders were usually bi-vocational, Peter's warning was that elders not use their position to seek the trade of the church in business matters. (How many businessmen have joined "First Church" primarily to climb the social and economic ladder?). Peter's warning also suggests that money did occasionally go along with the ministry of elder, and being "in it for the money" was not a good reason to be an elder! Yet another way to look at Peter's words is to see them as a caution for the elder to be willing to forgo potentially lucrative business ventures and instead give his time to serving as an elder.

**SYNTHESIS**

First, Jesus commanded that those who preach the gospel (evangelists) should make their living from the gospel. Paul, in an illustration, applied this same principle to apostles (1Co 9). Finally, it was applied to qualified elders (1Ti 5), using the same arguments found in 1Co 9. Ac 20 is addressed to elders in general. In general, elders are to be bi-vocational and will thus be in a position of giving monetarily to the church, rather than receiving from it. The exception to this generalization is 1Ti 5, written with reference to those elders who not only "rule well" but who also "labor in the word and doctrine" (NKJV). Though all elders are worthy of honor (1Th 5:12-13), some elders are worthy of double honor. This "double" honor most likely is a reference to financial support from the church. And, regardless of how an elder earns income (secular or sacred), he is to give generously to the needy. Blending Ac 20 with 1Ti 5 would also suggest that even those elders worthy of double honor (financial support) be willing and trained to work some secular vocation if local conditions require it (i.e., times of economic depression, poverty-stricken third world countries, very small churches, etc).

**Cautions**

1. Suggesting that the church is obligated to support those elders deemed worthy of "double honor" does not mean that these elders are somehow higher in rank than the other elders. One elder may be more gifted than another, or more influential, but there is no such thing in the NT as an official "senior" elder, nor of a hierarchy of elders.

2. To be avoided are elders (especially those worthy of double honor) who dominate the 1Co 14 meeting. If an elder receives financial support that enables him to study the Word, it's possible that he will have so much more to teach, and be expected to do so, that the other brothers won't feel as free to teach. That would squelch the priesthood of believers and violate 1Co 14:26. Such meetings are not to be pastor-centered. Instead, a gifted elder's in-depth teachings could come during a mid-week Bible study or apostolic-type meeting.

3. The "pastor-teacher" mentioned in Ep 4 is not somehow "over" all the churches of a city. Instead, he is the servant to all the churches of the city. As Beresford Job would say, there is to be no "big cheese" in charge.

4. Despite the evidence that qualified elders may make their livings from their ministries, there is to be no clergy-laity distinction. Authority resides in the church as a whole, not with its leaders. The leaders are to be humble servants, not lords. Rusty Entrekin warns: "Although we know that pastor-teachers are supposed to be servants and not in a special 'clergy' class, those who are not pastor-teachers will still have a tendency to regard them that way, especially because of our modern institutional church mind-set regarding professional pastors. Even if the pastor teacher doesn't think that way about himself initially, if he doesn't watch himself, he could very easily begin to gradually, perhaps imperceptibly, adopt that mind-set. Since the godly, sincere, and vibrant believers of the late first century and early second century church fell victim to this mind set, just think of how easily we could today, with the peer pressure of conventional "wisdom," centuries of traditions, and lukewarm spirituality encouraging us to do so! We need to be very, very careful not only to guard against the priesthood being robbed of their God-given rights, but also to exhort them not to give their rights away."

CONCLUSION

What can be concluded about the idea of full-time church workers?

1. There is no historical pattern in the NT either for or against full-time elders. It is silent.

2. There is a general command in Ac 20 for elders to follow Paul's example of supplying their own needs so as to be in a position of giving silver and gold and clothing to the church, rather than receiving from it.

3. All elders are worthy of honor (esteem), 1Th 5.

4. Qualified elders, those who rule and teach well, are worthy of "double honor" (financial support, 1Ti 5).

5. Elders are not to be motivated by the desire for "sordid gain" from their ministry (i.e., not just in it for the money, nor using the office to gain sales contacts or clients), 1Pe 5.

6. We need to financially support those who are evangelists, apostles, teachers, and elders, 1Co 9. It is the NT pattern to give to support people, not property. Give your money toward areas that God thinks are important.

— Steve Atkerson

# *14*
## *EVANGELISM*

---

We consider the last words of an individual to be of utmost importance. Family members will crowd around a dying man's bed to catch his last words and then recall them again and again for years to come. Well, I suggest that the last words of Jesus Christ before He ascended to heaven were of utmost importance. He gives them to us in all four gospel accounts and in the book of Acts.

**Mt 28:18-20**: "All authority has been given to Me in heaven and on earth. Go therefore and make disciples of all the nations, baptizing them in the name of the Father and the Son and the Holy Spirit, teaching them to observe all that I commanded you; and lo, I am with you always, even to the end of the age."

**Mk 16:15-16**: "Go into all the world and preach the gospel to all creation. He who has believed and has been baptized shall be saved; but he who has disbelieved shall be condemned."

**Lk 24:46-48**: "Thus it is written, that the Christ should suffer and rise again from the dead the third day; and that repentance for forgiveness of sins should be proclaimed in His name to all the nations, beginning from Jerusalem. You are witness of these things. And behold I am sending forth the promise of My Father upon you; but you are to stay in the city until you are clothed with power from on high."

**Jn 20:21**: "Peace be with you; as the Father has sent Me, I also send you."

**Ac 1:8**: "…but you shall receive power when the Holy Spirit has come upon you; and you shall be My witnesses both in Jerusalem, and in all Judea and Samaria, and even to the remotest part of the earth."

Notice that in every case Jesus emphasizes the responsibility of the apostles to extend His kingdom. They are to make disciples of all the nations, preach the gospel to all creation, proclaim repentance for forgiveness of sins to all the nations, be sent by Jesus Christ just as He was sent by His Father, and be witnesses to the remotest part of the earth. Jesus gives the same basic message in five different ways in order that the apostles would have no doubt as to what their job was after He left. He left these words ringing in their ears. He had one thing He wanted to impress indelibly on their minds. It was as if He was saying, "If you forget everything else I've taught you, you must never forget this!" These texts form the marching orders for the Church until Christ returns.

Those of us who meet in home churches must deal responsibly with these final words of Jesus Christ. Theoretically, we should have an advantage over those who meet in more traditional settings. Since we do not typically use our money to hire a pastor or pay for a mortgage on a building, we should have all the finances necessary to do the work of evangelism in our city. Additionally, the house church model is much easier to reproduce than the traditional church. In order to plant another house church we don't need to hire a seminary trained individual, and build a special religious edifice complete with cross, stained glass windows, pulpit, pews and organ. All we really need to plant a house church is a handful of people who love Jesus Christ and want to follow Him together. On the other hand, the whole dynamic of a house church can work against the command of Christ to reach out with His gospel. Often, when someone comes into a house church they enjoy the rich and intimate fellowship with other believers so much, that they tend to focus on that to the neglect of equally important matters, like evangelism, discipleship and church planting. However, we must not let that happen to us. Our churches must not only have an inward nurturing thrust. They must also have an outward missionary thrust.

Too often the church has a fortress mentality. We see the power of Satan and his demons, and wanting to protect ourselves from the power and pollution of sin, we retreat and cloister together in fear. However, instead of finding ourselves on the defensive, we ought to be on the offensive! Jesus said that the gates of Hades would not overpower His church (Mt 16:18). In this passage the church is on the offensive, and hell is on the defensive! I understand Jesus to mean that as the church boldly, and aggressively invades Satan's kingdom with the gospel of Jesus Christ, the devil will not be able to successfully oppose our onslaught. We will prevail. We have the power and authority to invade the kingdom of darkness with the truth of the gospel, and hell can't stop us. Let this truth from the lips of Christ encourage and embolden you to new evangelistic exploits!

If all this is true, how should our house churches engage in the task of reaching the lost and planting new churches? Let's take a look at where and how the early church evangelized to get some direction for our own churches.

WHERE DID THE EARLY CHURCH EVANGELIZE?

Often churches today seek to evangelize by inviting non-Christians to one of their meetings. A popular approach is to gear the Sunday church service towards non-Christians by having professional music and drama, and practical messages directed towards the nonbeliever in areas such as finances, stress, work, and family. It is hoped that unbelievers will be attracted to Christ through such means. After they have been converted, they are encouraged to attend a Bible study during the week where they can grow in their faith. However, the New Testament approach is almost completely opposite. Instead of inviting the lost to church meetings, most New Testament evangelism took place during the week as believers came into contact with unbelievers, or as apostolic workers proclaimed Christ in public places. Church meetings were designed for the edification of believers, not the conversion of unbelievers (1Co 14:3,5,12,17,26). Of course, on occasion unbelievers did attend church meetings (1Co 14:24-25), but the meetings were not designed for them, but rather the strengthening of the church. It seems that the Biblical model is to proclaim Christ to others as the Lord provides opportunity for our witness, and when someone comes to faith in Christ, to then invite them to begin meeting with other believers in our corporate gatherings.

HOW DID THE EARLY CHURCH EVANGELIZE?

The early church took Jesus' words at face value and sought to obey them. They did so in two different ways. Speaking in broad, general categories, apostles (church planters) and evangelists sought to reach those they did not know through public proclamation, while the other members of the church sought to reach the lost through daily interaction with people they did know. Apostolic workers proclaimed Christ in synagogues, market places, and riversides (Ac 13:5,14; 17:17; 16;13). The rest of the church on the other hand, witnessed primarily through their daily, regular contact with unbelievers. That's why Paul wrote to them and said, "Conduct yourselves with wisdom toward outsiders, making the most of the opportunity. Let your speech always be with grace, seasoned as it were, with salt, so that you may know how you should respond to each person" (Col.3:5-6). Peter exhorts likewise, "...but sanctify Christ as Lord in your hearts, always being ready to make a defense to everyone who asks you to give an account for the hope that is in you, yet with gentleness and reverence" (1Pe 3:15). Early church members were to *respond* to outsiders, and be always ready to make a defense to everyone *who asks*. These passages seem to indicate that the early Christians usually witnessed to the life transforming power of the gospel to those they already knew (life-style evangelism), whereas the apostles (church planters) took a more aggressive approach in proclaiming Christ to those they did not know.

What implications does this have for how our house churches should reach out to the lost? It means that those in our churches whom God has gifted and called to work in evangelism (evangelists and church planters) will look for venues to present the gospel of Christ to those they don't know. Perhaps they will engage in open air preaching, street evangelism, door to door witnessing, and tract distribution. Perhaps they will be given opportunities to speak at various events and functions. Because I am a bluegrass banjo player I have been given several opportunities to preach the gospel to largely secular audiences at concerts and festivals.

On the other hand, other members of the congregation should be praying and looking for opportunities to speak a word for Christ to those they interact with, like classmates, neighbors, work mates, relatives, customers or other acquaintances. Additionally we need to regularly seek to put ourselves in places where we can interact with non-Christians. We can join a neighborhood watch program, civic group, or square dancing group to meet people. We can open our homes during the holidays and invite our neighbors in. We can invite unbelievers into our homes for dinner. We can start an investigative Bible study for any of our unsaved friends who are open to learning what the Bible has to say. We can ask our unbelieving friends what we can be praying for in their lives. I have been surprised to find out how many of our neighbors were actually lonely people and welcomed a loving friendship. When God gives an opportunity for us to befriend an unbeliever, we need to just be ourselves, and let our light shine. The opportunities abound to love people and thus make an eternal difference in their lives.

In addition, our churches should pray for and give generously to those God has gifted and called to evangelize and plant churches. The apostle Paul often urged local congregations to pray for him in his evangelistic and church planting labors (Ep 6:19-20; Col.4:3-4). In the texts just cited, Paul is urging believers to pray for him that God would give him boldness to proclaim the mystery of the gospel, and that God would open to him a door for the word that he could speak forth the mystery of Christ. Furthermore, Paul consistently commended those churches who generously gave of their finances to support his evangelistic work (Php 4:14-19; 2Co 8:1-5). Let's pray for and give to those whom God has raised up as evangelists and church planters today.

Out of all the people the church witnesses to, there will be some who God has prepared to receive Christ and be saved. What then? Well, the person who led the individual to Christ, if possible, should begin to disciple them by spending time with them, encouraging them, answering questions they have about how to live for God, and providing an example for them in serving Christ. As God saves new believers we can either add them to the existing church, or begin a new church plant. Since house churches have a built in size limitation (as many as can fit in a house), you will probably start to experience difficulties meeting together when the numbers approach 35 or 40 people. At that point plan to plant a new church! You can plant the new church either by splitting the previous church in two, or hiving off a few people and starting a new church plant, while leaving the previous church pretty much intact. I personally prefer the latter method. When people begin to form strong friendships in a church, it can be traumatic to tear them apart. It may be much less stressful to take a few new believers and a brother gifted in church planting and have them begin meeting in a new location. The church planter can begin to teach these new believers how to function as a church, and how to reach their social circle with the gospel of Christ. Hopefully, over time, God will raise up from these new converts mature brothers who can serve as elders to shepherd the flock. The church planter is now free to devote himself to planting a new church, and so the process begins all over again.

Oh may God stir those of us involved in house churches to labor to fulfill the Great Commission that Jesus might receive glory and His kingdom extend around the world!

— Brian Anderson

*Some believers are supernaturally gifted in evangelism and/or church planting. Their existence and ministry is a NT pattern, especially in pioneer areas. However, it does not follow that every new church must be started by a bona fide church planter, else it is not a true NT church. While their ministry is a great help in the plant of a new church, it is not essential, particularly in areas where the gospel has already been preached and the church firmly established. — Editor*

# 15

# HEALTHY ASSEMBLY LIFE

Believers who begin to practice *ekklesia* outside of traditional churches usually face a number of obstacles. Obviously, everyone brings their past churchy baggage with them to some degree. Folks can often see the problems with how most churches try to do things, but they are not always sure how to avoid such pitfalls in the fresh setting of home gatherings. In this chapter I would like to set forth some basic, fundamental perspectives that past experience tells me will go a long way toward helping the saints to get started on the right foot. First, we will look at the foundation we must work from, then we will examine some very practical issues about getting along with one another and working out problems together.

## WHAT DO WE BUILD ON?

Given the propensity of human traditions to multiply and block the truth, it is important for believers to be sure that their practice of church is built on the correct foundation. A search of the New Testament reveals that there is only one foundation for the *ekklesia* and that is Jesus Christ Himself — His unique person, His redemptive work, and His authoritative words (1Co 3:11; 15:3-4; Mt.7:28-29; 17:5). In terms of what Jesus taught it is clear to see what He viewed as central for the New Covenant community. On the eve of His death, after He had washed the disciples' feet, He announced without ambiguity, "A new commandment I give to you, that you love one another. As I have loved you, that you also love one another. By this all people will know that you are my disciples, if you have love one to another" (Jn 13:34-35). Every outworking of church life must flow out of a one-another love that imitates what the Lord did for us on the cross (Jn 15:12-13).

## WHERE DID OUR EXODUS OCCUR?

It is vital to see the precise parallel at this point between the Old and New Covenants. Both covenants were based upon the Lord's action in history to separate to Himself a people. Israel was separated to God by the Exodus out of Egypt; the *ekklesia* was separated to God by the Exodus accomplished by Christ in Jerusalem (Lk 9:31). The moral demand on Israel was first prefaced by mention of God's mighty arm: "I am the Lord your God who brought you out of Egypt, out of the land of slavery" (Ex 20:2). The moral demand upon the New Covenant people is rooted in Christ's work on Golgotha, "as I have loved you." The pattern is clear — the redemptive event (the indicative) is the basis for the required lifestyle (the imperatives) of the covenant peoples. That is to say, the event that saves us also commands us how to live. Douglas Webster said that, "Understanding the nature of Christ coincides with living out the ethics of Jesus . . . . The Christian ethic is exclusively dependent upon Christian redemption . . . . Jesus' cross is planted squarely at the center of the believer's existence, providing both the means of salvation and the challenge of a new life-style" (*A Passion for Christ: An Evangelical Christology*, Zondervan, 1987, pp.52,149,153).

If you look at books on Christian Ethics you will discover that most of them end up being expositions of the Ten Commandments, as if ethical fullness can only be found in Exodus 20. In such volumes the "new commandment" and its implications are almost never given any attention. To cite a glaring example, in Patrick Fairbairn's massive *The Revelation of Law in Scripture*, he devotes a great deal of space to the Ten Commandments, but says almost nothing about the "new command" in John 13. In the history of theology more attention has fallen on the Old Covenant ethics based on the Egyptian Exodus than on the New Covenant ethics flowing out of the Exodus Christ carried out in Jerusalem (Lk 9:31). Perhaps this accounts for why "church" traditionally, in certain key areas, has been shaped more by Old Covenant images than New Covenant revelation.

In light of John 13 it is imperative that we build upon the foundation articulated by Christ. The New Covenant was sealed and inaugurated by the shedding of His blood. On the eve of His death as the spotless lamb of God, He announced that a new commandment was inseparably connected to His New Exodus. A question that must be answered is, "What makes this commandment 'new'?" The command to love was ancient and revealed many times in the Old Testament. What makes it "new" is uncovered in the Lord's words, "*as I have loved you.*" A new redemptive event brings with it a singular command to love one another, out of which flows all the many other imperatives embedded in the New Covenant — "if you love me, keep my commandments."

The specific focus of the new commandment is *one another*. This shows that Christian ethics primarily relates to *body ethics*. At the core of the New Testament is a concern for the *Ekklesia* to live out the implications of the "new man," which Christ created on the cross, making peace in a priesthood where there is neither Jew nor Greek, bond nor free, male nor female. As Paul Lehmann observes, "Christian ethics is *koinonia ethics*," and the *ekklesia* is a context where *maturity*, and not mere morality, is spawned (*Ethics in A Christian Context*, Harper, 1963, pp.47,54). Our ecclesiology, therefore, must be rooted in the *New Covenant* which has been put into effect as binding, and our relations as brothers and sisters must be bathed in the *new commandment* to love one another as He loved us at Calvary.

### "Accept One Another / Admonish One Another"

After being a Christian for fifteen years, around 1980 I began to struggle with a problem that occurs with tragic frequency in Bible-believing circles. I saw church split after church split. I saw brethren biting and devouring one another. I thought in my heart, "How can the New Testament, which puts so much emphasis on love and unity, become the source for so much division and strife?" Somewhere in the midst of my personal turmoil, the Lord brought me to the two-fold perspective of Paul in Romans 15. It does not, of course, bring an immediate resolution to every possible scenario we will face. However, I strongly believe that to the degree that we can practice this two-fold dimension of assembly life, we will go a long way toward avoiding the ugliness that, unfortunately, has come to mark much that bears the name Christian.

In the context Paul has dealt with the sticky reality that the early church had to face early on – Jews and Gentiles were brought together as a "new man," and they were meeting together in the same homes. Paul, of course, did not opt for the easy thing to do, namely, have Jewish believers meet in one place, and the Gentile believers meet somewhere else. The only consistent outworking of the Gospel was for *the two radically different ethnic groups to meet together* because Jesus on the cross brought the two together, thereby making peace (Ep 2:12-18). This was a volatile situation, and Paul faces it head-on in Romans 14-15.

So after dealing with how Jewish and Gentile saints should show love to one another in areas like foods, drinks and days, Paul comes to the conclusion of the matter in Romans 15:7 – "Accept one another, then, just as Christ accepted you, in order to bring praise to God." Then in verse 14 we discover the flip side of this exhortation to accept each other – "I myself am convinced, my brothers, that you yourselves are full of goodness, complete in knowledge and competent to instruct one another." In these two verses a tension is revealed that we must all wrestle with: how can we pursue truth together without destroying our fellowship, and how can we pursue fellowship together without avoiding Christ's truth?

Churches tend to illustrate the pendulum swing – they either pursue truth in an atmosphere without love and caring (which results in witch-hunts), or they emphasize acceptance and love with little interest in Christ's revealed will (which results in gushy sentimentality). Why do we sever what God has joined together? Why can't we cultivate and encourage an atmosphere of acceptance in which we will learn to speak the truth to one another in love? Our tendency is to reject other Christians who disagree with our understanding of Scripture in what we regard as crucial issues. Or, there is the tendency to so underscore acceptance that there is no concern for revealed truth. *To fully accept one another in the bonds of the Gospel and to instruct one another in an atmosphere of acceptance is a tension we must face and work out.*

Growth, according to Paul, can occur only when we speak the truth to one another in love (Ep 4:15; Jn 17:17). Elliot Johnson rightly observes, "In a sense, evangelicals have lived with an interpretational truce. While we agree on doctrinal 'essentials' we have also agreed to not talk very seriously about issues of disagreement. Yet Paul charted God's strategy for Christian growth [in Ep 4:12-13]. In order to reach unity we need some way to talk about our different interpretations and to evaluate these differences" ("Author's Intention & Biblical Interpretation," Position Paper given in Chicago at the International Council on Biblical Inerrancy, 1982, pp.1-2).

The problem in most configurations of believers is that the very rationale for the group's existence rules out the possibility of certain "truths" being discussed. The "truth" is already defined in terms of some pre-determined boundaries. I suggest that this kind of behavior is childish and makes a mockery of the Holy Spirit and the Gospel. When we face new issues from the Word are we willing to *work together, study together, pray together and even fast together* in order to seek the Lord's mind and come to greater agreement? Most of us are ready to separate from other brethren at the drop of a hat. But it takes a commitment to the truth and to the brothers and sisters to be willing to work matters out.

SEEKING TRUTH TOGETHER IN FELLOWSHIP

In 1981 a brother sent me some material from Vernard Eller's 1964 doctoral thesis. It was like dew from heaven. It put into words what I had begun to see emerge from Romans 15:7 and 14. It provided a singularly important grid that will help any group get started in the right direction. When groups fall apart I believe the root causes can be traced back to a failure to practice the vital perspectives Eller has isolated. What follows are some of his key thoughts that echo the two-fold vantage point of Romans 15:

•*Previous Commitment to Follow Scripture* '— Such an assembly must come to the Scriptures having previously made the commitment to obey and follow as literally and completely as possible whatever leading may be discovered therein.

•*Centrality of Love* — Such an assembly, above all, must preserve the love for one another, without which any religious insight, no matter how correct it may be technically, loses its truth.

•*Instruct in An Atmosphere of Love* — Such an assembly will respect and maintain brotherhood with all sincere seekers of truth [Rom.15:7], though at the same time, they will see it as their Christian duty to point out what they feel to be the errors in the other's thinking [Rom.15:14].

•*Seeking Truth Without Fracturing Fellowship* — A dialectic is in operation here: The preservation of fellowship is of supreme value; however, uniformity, or unanimity, in the truth is also of high value. The pressure toward unanimity dare not be allowed to destroy fellowship, but neither dare the joys of fellowship be allowed to stifle the search for the point of concord that marks the truth . . . . If this dialectical balance be patiently maintained, the Spirit can and will eventually bring about unanimity – while in the process enhancing rather than destroying fellowship.

•*Humility and Openness Necessary* — Much more important than *having* the truth is being in a position to *receive* the truth; thus, the life of the church always must be open-ended toward God. (*Searching Together*, Spring, 1983, pp.13-14).

If every assembly would walk in the power of the Spirit according to the ways described above, we would see a lot less rancor and a lot more unity in love and truth. The problem is, of course, that it is people like you and I who make up the parts of each *ekklesia*. We are all very capable of putting ourselves and our agendas ahead of others. This reality underscores the importance of each part of the body being *committed* to loving one another fervently. When physical families have problems they don't run away from each other. Hopefully, there is a commitment present that will stick it out during the process of resolving issues. How much more in the spiritual body of Christ should we be willing to persevere with one another in anticipation of the Lord by His Spirit enhancing our fellowship as we speak the truth in love?

## "AGREE WITH ONE ANOTHER" (1CO 1:10)

No human family can function indefinitely without having to face a conflict or problem. Likewise, in Christ's family there will be problems that must be resolved. Indeed, much of what was written in the New Testament had to do with correcting errors of teaching and practice among the saints. What guidelines does the New Testament give for working through the bumpy times that any congregation will inevitably face? 1 Corinthians 1:10 reveals some critical apostolic teaching in this regard.

First, it can be noted that Paul directs his exhortation to the "brethren." These were believers in a city who *maintained an ongoing relationship with one another in the bonds of Christ.* They were committed to one another because of their common interest in the Gospel. It is this deep mutual fellowship (*koinonia*) in Christ that provides the backdrop for Paul's approach to them with correction. Larry Crabb notes a vital perspective that emerges from this consideration, "Change takes place when *truth is presented in relationship.* Perhaps a relationship of deep regard and empathetic concern is the *context* for change, creating an atmosphere in which the truth of God can be heard nondefensively and thus penetrate more deeply . . . . to be healthy, *a church must present truth in the context of encouraging relationships"* (*Encouragement: The Key to Caring*, Zondervan, 1984, pp.84,91).

This insight reflects what we saw in Romans 15:7. A loving, caring, accepting atmosphere must be the context for speaking the truth to each other in love (Rom.15:14). What reason would we have to think that Gospel truth will take deep root in a setting which reflected instead the modified line from the old song, "Where seldom is heard, an encouraging word"?

Next, Paul confronts the Corinthians with a very serious problem. Paul had a number of issues with them, but this is the one at the top of his list. They were clustering around gifted personalities, and by such schism were ruining the image of an undivided Christ. "Each one of you is saying, 'I'm of Paul; and I'm of Apollos; and I'm of Peter; and I'm of Christ.'" This sinful division was already occurring and had driven the saints apart from one another.

To solve this problem Paul appeals to them "to agree" about the wickedness of this situation. If they "agreed" then the divisions could no longer exist. The participle *katartismenoi* used in verse 10 is significant. It is from the same verb used in Ep 4:12, translated there as "equip" or "prepare." It is the verb used when the disciples were "mending" their nets (Mt 4:21; Mk 1:19). We could loosely translate the verb, "mending with a view toward rendering something as functional again." This idea also emerges again in Galatians 6:1, "*restore* such a one..."

As used in the context of 1Co 1:10, we can see an important implication of being "perfectly united in mind and thought." While we are not given any of the details as to how they worked this out, at a minimum we can say that the Corinthians had to work through this matter until the breach was "mended" and they finally "agreed." *A process which results in unity is in view.* They were already split apart, so in order for the torn garment to be repaired they had to: (1) take the apostolic instruction; (2) come back together; (3) face and discuss the word of the Lord together; (4) repent of their sins; and (5) be restored again to their original oneness.

The utterly amazing fact is that, even with all their problems, *Paul assumes that the assembly has the spiritual resources to overcome their waywardness.* Many posit that the problem-solving abilities Paul presupposes will only work among mature churches. But this is a bogus suggestion. Corinth was in many ways a very *immature* assembly, but Paul still expects them, for example, to deal with immorality in their midst (1Co 5) and to resolve their disputes internally without going to unbelieving courts (1Co 6).

The apostles taught that within the New Covenant community *all* were anointed by the Holy Spirit who enabled them to "test" and "discern" what the will of God might be (1Jn 2:20,27; 4:1; 1Th :21). The *ekklesia*, therefore, is first of all a *discerning community*, able to "bind and loose," and thus is also a *decision-making community*. The very word chosen to earmark the New Covenant people of God, *ekklesia*, is taken from the secular political realm, not from a religious context. *Ekklesia* referred to a group of people with common interests getting together to accomplish certain business. It would be very similar to the town meetings that took place in developing America in the 1800's. John H. Yoder observes that, "The word *ekklesia* itself . . . does not refer to a specifically religious meeting, nor to a particular organization: it rather mean the "assembly," the gathering of a people into a meeting *for deliberation* or for a public pronouncement . . . . The church is where, *because there Jesus is confessed as Christ*, people are empowered to speak to one another in God's name . . . . It is only in the local face-to-face meeting, with brothers and sisters, who know one another well, that this process can take place of which Jesus says that what has been decided stands decided in heaven" ("Binding & Loosing," *Concern #14*, Feb. 1967, pp.2ff.; cf. *TDNT*, IV, p.336).

As you reflect on the New Testament epistles, it is quite striking that church leaders are not addressed separately, as if some special decision-making authority resided in them  Instead, Paul directs his writings to the *entire assembly*.  For example, he does not rebuke the elders at Corinth for failing to deal with the immoral person or for not resolving the disputes among the brethren.  He puts the nexus of responsibility on the *whole congregation* to carry out Christ's revealed will.

Paul's approach flies in the face of the traditional decision-making method, which views "the pastor," or a body of leaders, as the source of decisions.  Abraham Kuyper, for instance, removed the "right to judge" from the congregation and asserted that "the administrative authority over the church rests not with the members, but properly with the presbyters" ("Pamphlet on The Reformation of the Church," *The Standard Bearer*, Oct. 1979, p.14).  Jay Adams avers that "take it to the church" means "take it to the elders," who then forgive or excommunicate (*Ready to Forgive*, Pres. & Reformed, pp.3-4).  Such an interpretation is arbitrary, informed more by presuppositions than by the text itself.  Elders will certainly be a part of the "discerning" process in the body, but the New Testament will not sustain the notion that *elders are the process itself.*  The truth is, there is very little focus on elders in the New Testament, compared to the at least fifty-eight "one-another" imperatives found therein.

Both times Jesus uses *ekklesia* to identify His New Covenant people, He attaches "binding and loosing" to its function (Mt16:19; 18:18).  This clearly indicates that we need to significantly broaden our ideas of what is entailed in doing "church."  Traditionally, doing church means going to a building, sitting in a pew, singing some songs, putting some money in a plate, hearing a sermon, shaking the pastor's hand, and heading home to get your roast out of the oven. Most fundamentally, however, *ekklesia* means doing the whole gamut of kingdom activities with other committed believers in a local congregation.  We are not used to thinking of resolving disputes within the body as "church," but the essence of practicing *ekklesia* involves *problem-solving* and *decision-making* in an atmosphere of loving acceptance where Christ's truth can be spoken in love.

It behooves us, therefore, to realize that it is expected of assemblies to "agree with one another" and to be "perfectly united in mind and thought"  This does not mean that we must have unanimity regarding every doctrinal nuance, but it does mean that we must be ready to work things out with our brethren as required in light of apostolic teaching.  Paul was not surprised when congregations had problems, but he was upset when they failed to work through their problems together as a body. Here is a question each of us needs to face: when the inevitable day comes in my assembly that a problem surfaces, am I going to run and hide from it, or am I going to stand with the body and do my part to be part of its resolution? Real *ekklesia* requires hard work and commitment, but we must never forget that Jesus' presence by the Spirit, persistent prayer, preferring others ahead of ourselves, and fervent love are where the battles are won.

### "HONOR ONE ANOTHER ABOVE YOURSELVES" (Ro 12:10)

One of the most staggering goals of Christ's work is set forth is 2Co 5:15, "those who live should no longer live for themselves, but for Him who died for them and was raised again." One of the unending lessons of discipleship is to take up our cross daily and follow Christ, to consciously by the Spirit's power stop living for ourselves and serve Him. In terms of our life in the body of Christ, one of the key ways we demonstrate a selfless life is to put others' needs ahead of our own.

Think about it. If each believer was preferring others ahead of oneself, everybody's needs would be met. We would all be looking out for each other. No one would be forgotten. It sounds so simple, but we all know that body life does not work out that smoothly because each of us struggles with putting ourselves ahead of others.

In terms of our life together as believers, and in light of our responsibility to work things out in the body, one of the central ways we manifest non-self-centered living is by *listening to the concerns and burdens of others.* James 1:19 says, "let everyone be quick to hear, and slow to speak and slow to anger."

Some commentators see in James' remark a corrective to what was transpiring in early Christian gatherings. Curtis Vaughn and Earl Kelly note that, "There may be an illusion [in James 1:19] to the free and unstructured worship of the early Christian assemblies" (*James: A Study Guide*, Zondervan, 1960, p.35). Further, "It is possible that contentious Christian babes were taking advantage of the informal style of worship in the early Christian church to produce wrangling" (*James: A Primer for Christian Living*, Presbyterian & Reformed, 1974, p.69).

The point is that in our dealings with one another each of us must first of all "be quick to hear." Obviously, in any configuration of brethren there will be those will want to talk a lot, those who are very reticent, and others inbetween. Those who have the gift of gab should take to heart James' admonition, "be slow to speak." They should prefer others ahead of themselves, and be sure that they do not stifle the input of others, either by dominating the discussion, or by coming across in such a dogmatic tone that no one feels up to contributing their thoughts. The verbally timid should be encouraged to share their insights by the rest of the group, realizing that "each one of us" has the potential of adding edifying content to the meeting (1Co 14:26). As William Barclay observes about the meeting described in 1 Corinthians. 14, "The really notable thing about an early Church service must have been that almost everyone came feeling that he had both the privilege and obligation of contributing something to it . . . . Obviously this had its dangers for it is clear that in Corinth there were those who were too fond of the sound of their own voices" (*The Letters to the Corinthians*, Westminster Press, pp.149-150).

In light of the exhortation for each of us to be "quick to hear," what are some vital attitudes that we must cultivate in our body relationships?

1. *We must be open to learn from brethren in various traditions.* We all tend to stick to some party-line and turn our heads away from information outside of our comfort zone. A.N. Groves wrote in 1833 concerning his relationship with J.N. Darby, "I do not think we ought to propose to be modeled *unlike* every sect, but simply to be like Christ; let us neither seek nor fear a name. *I wish rather to have from every sect what every sect may have from Christ*" (Roy Coad, *A History of the Brethren Movement*, pp.114-115).

Are we willing to "listen" to multiple sources and discern from them what might help us discover the mind of Christ? Are we really open to be challenged by others to search the Scriptures and see what is indeed so? Thomas Dubay notes in this regard: "Since no one of us mortals, affected as we are with original sin, is perfectly pure in his desire for truth, no one of us is exempt from some degree of closemindedness. It is only our God who is truth than can cure our reluctance to embrace all of his truth, however he speaks it" ("Communication in Community," *Searching Together*, Winter, 1985, p.11).

2. *"We need to be humble,"* says Dubay, "small in our own estimation. Finding the solution to a mathematical problem is possible without humility, but finding God's will is impossible without this virtue. James 4:6 tells us that God resists the proud but gives grace (and light) to the humble" ("Communication," p.11). Whenever a group of believers bathed in humility gather together, great things can be expected; but, as James 3:16 notes, where there is "envy and selfish ambition, there you find disorder and every evil practice." The truly humble put others ahead of themselves. They pay attention to what they hear

from others.

3. *We must always have a "willingness to be changed by what is going to be said (without, of course, sacrificing genuine principles).* One listens wholly only if he is willing to modify his present position if the evidence warrants it. People who are set in their thoughts and determined not to change their behavior do not listen to contrary evidences" (Dubay, p.11). If we confess that we do not know anything as we ought, then we will be open to new light from our brethren. We must listen to possible new evidence that has escaped our attention. As Eller noted, the church must always be open-ended toward God's truth in Christ.

4. *We must "grow in awareness that the person speaking is important, even precious, "God's beloved" (Rom.1:7).* We pay attention to important people. To the proud person others are not important and so he is not inclined to take them seriously. Even more, we value the opinions of those we love. If I do not really care what my brother thinks, I had better doubt that I love my brother" (Dubay, p.11). I have seen so many cases in assemblies where those who articulate things with razor-sharp logic bulldoze over the "little person," and pooh-pooh any concerns they have. You may think that a question or concern coming from another is immature, or ill-timed, or very low on your list of priorities, but if you really love that person you must give your ears and heart to that fellow-believer who is precious to Christ. We must highly esteem the input of every part of the body, or we run the risk of missing the voice of Jesus in our midst. In Christ's body we are instructed to heap more honor on those parts that seem to be weaker and less honorable (1Co 12:22-24).

A huge chunk of not living for ourselves, but for Christ, is displayed in how we defer to one another in the body of Christ. Without apology I say that to the degree a committed body of believers by God's grace follows the perspectives set forth in this article, they will fare well and be able to tackle the inevitable bumps that come in the course of assembly life. If these perspectives are forgotten, neglected, or rejected, then a body will more than likely self-destruct. Functioning together in the *ekklesia* is like holding a bird in your hand. If you hold it too tightly you will kill it. If you hold it too loosely it will fly away. If believers are fueled by the love Christ had for them on the cross – "as I have loved you" – then they can successfully keep the bird alive by loving one another fervently.

After considering what has been said about body life, you may be thinking: "There is just one thing wrong with the biblical view of the church which we have been sketching: *it does not seem to exist.* The easo.. tt

definition is fine, but the phenomenon it describes is missing" (John H. Yoder, "A Light to All Nations," *Concern #9*, March, 1961, p.17).

The fact that we are so far from where we should be is a valid cause for concern. But the truth that these attitudes and perspectives are the obvious will of Christ by the Spirit must give us great confidence that they can become realities in our assemblies.

"Lord Jesus, please enable us to give ourselves to the life of love you have revealed in your Word."

— Jon Zens

FURTHER RESOURCES

•"Coming to Truth in Fellowship with Others" [11 Articles], *ST*, Spring, 1983, 48pp. ($3.00)

•Dubay, Thomas. "Communication in Community," *ST*, Winter, 1985, pp.1-14. ($2.00)

•Hammett, Rosine & Loughlin Sofield, "Developing Healthy Christian Community," *ST*, Autumn, 1986, pp.2-16. ($2.00)

•Zens, Jon. "'As I Have Loved You': The Starting Point of Christian Obedience," *ST*, Summer, 1980, pp.4-26. ($3.00)

•Zens, Jon. "Building Up the Body: One Man or One Another?," *ST*, Summer, 1981, pp.10-33. ($3.00)

•Zens, Jon. Four Plenary Sessions at the 2001 Southern House Church Conference: "As I Have Loved You," "Accept One Another/Admonish One Another," "Agree With One Another," "Honor One Another." 4 Cassettes. ($13.00)

•Zens, Jon. "'This Is My Beloved Son, Hear Him': The Foundation for New Covenant Ethics & Ecclesiology," *ST*, 25:1-3, 97pp. ($6.00)

*The above materials are available from Searching Together, Box 377, Taylors Falls, MN 55084*

# 16

# CHURCH DISCIPLINE

The term "church discipline" often conjures up memories of heretics being tortured on the rack, beheaded, or burned at the stake. In the Massachusetts Bay Colony, "witches" were hung, drunks were locked in pillories, and adulteresses had to wear the letter "A" on their breasts to mark them for life. Furthermore, the topic of church discipline is rarely discussed and even more rarely practiced in the modern church. Where church discipline is discussed, one often hears cries of "Judge not, lest ye be judged" or "Let he who has not sinned cast the first stone." In those few churches where it is practiced, often times it is left up to "the" pastor, a board of elders, or a diaconate to dismiss the offending church member. This is not the NT pattern.

Why is it that church discipline is rarely, if ever, practiced in our local churches today? Why are Christian marriages being ripped apart in record numbers? Why are Christians allowed to continue indefinitely in unreconciled relationships?

The apostle Paul, aware of the hazardous effects of unrepentant sin, admonishes the Corinthians, "Your boasting is not good. Don't you know that a little yeast works through the whole batch of dough? Get rid of the old yeast that you may be a new batch without yeast – as you really are. For Christ, our Passover lamb, has been sacrificed" (1Co 5:6-7). If we are to expect the blessing of God, we must with great zeal honor God in our congregations by faithfully disciplining unrepentant sinners (Nu 25). God is honored by properly administered church discipline and is greatly dishonored by its absence.

The size of most churches of the modern era often makes the practice of church discipline difficult. The best place for a tree to hide is in the forest. It is difficult, if not impossible, to be intimate with a large crowd of people and to know what issues are pressing in their lives. However, in the smaller house church, it is hard to hide. Sooner or later our sins will reveal themselves, and correction will be administered. The close community of the small home church lends itself to this practice of church discipline. It is not only easier to detect sin in a house church, but it can be easier for the offender to accept rebuke from people who know and love him.

In this chapter we will first examine the procedures for church discipline spoken by Jesus in Mt 18:15-20. Then, we will attempt to determine who the proper candidates for church discipline are and also how the church is to treat those individuals undergoing church discipline. Lastly, we will look at some common objections given for not practicing church discipline.

Because of the misconceptions of church discipline that many people have, it is essential that we examine what the Bible says concerning church discipline procedures. In the OT, discipline was often carried out by execution, banishment, or monetary restitution. It must be remembered, however, that Israel was a theocracy; i.e., governed by God. The Christian church slipped into a corruption of this pattern around the time of Constantine, after Christianity became the state religion of the Roman Empire. Many horrible practices occurred as a result of this unholy marriage between church and state. Athanasius of Alexandria was exiled from his home no less than six times because he defended the deity of Christ. Many died on the rack and at the stake under the Spanish Inquisition. John Bunyan was jailed twelve years in England for preaching without a license. This is not the NT pattern.

The procedure that should be carried out is as follows:

1. The offended brother should confront the offending brother alone.
2. If the offending brother does not repent, then the brother first offended confronts him again, this time with one or two more witnesses.
3. If the offending brother still does not repent, the offense is reported to the church.
4. If the offending brother does not repent after being confronted by the church, then the church does not associate with him. This is the fullest extent of the punishment, and never is the state to enforce this decision.
5. If the offending brother repents at any stage of this process, the church forgives him and the church discipline process stops at that point.

Matthew 18:15 states that the first step in church discipline is for the offended brother to go and confront the offending brother alone, and if he repents he has won his brother. Note that a "brother" committed the offense. The Greek word here is *adelphos*, meaning a member of the Christian community. It must be left up to God to judge those outside the church (1Co 5:13). That the offense represents a violation of the law of Christ is indicated by the Greek word *hamartano*, translated "trespasses" or "sins." This is not referring to disagreement over something such as how he cuts his hair, but to a real transgression of

Scripture. The offended brother is to "show him his fault." A one word synonym for this phrase would be "rebuke." The offended brother is to rebuke the offending brother privately. The first confrontation is to be a private matter. Then, Jesus says, if he hears you, you have gained or won your brother. This is the goal of any and all church discipline. If this happens, the process stops. It goes no further. Some of you may say, "Well, this goes on in my church all the time; we admonish each other frequently." Great! You are practicing the first step in church discipline.

In the event that your brother ignores you the first time, then you take witnesses with you, which is the second step in church discipline. This is a parallel to OT law. An Israeli could not be convicted of a capital crime unless there was more than one witness. The purpose of the witness is to corroborate every word spoken by the offended brother. This step prevents the "my word against yours" situation.

If the offending brother ignores both the offended brother and the witnesses, then the case is taken to the church (the church being defined as the local assembly). If this brother ignores even the whole church, then he is not to be associated with, which is the meaning of the phrase, "let him be to you as a heathen and a tax collector." Tax collectors and the Gentiles were seen as enemies. There are two points to note here: the corporate church carries out the final step of church discipline, and the local church is the final "court" where this case can be heard. To give to a pastor, board of elders or deacons the power to exercise this final step of church discipline is to give to one man or board too much power. Jesus gives that power to the local Christian assembly alone.

Who are the proper candidates for church discipline? While most Christians would agree that some form of church discipline is necessary for maintaining order and decency in the church, there is disagreement regarding when to apply the four steps of church discipline taught in Mt 18:15-20. In other words, what type(s) of "sin" did Jesus have in mind when he spoke in Mt 18? Verse 15 says, "If your brother sins against you, go and show him his fault, just between the two of you. If he listens to you, you have won your brother over." Notice that Jesus does not elaborate as to the nature of the sin in 18:15. He simply says, "If your brother has sinned against you, go and show him his fault." Paul, in 1Co 5, mentions several sins that would warrant the implementation of church discipline. Paul says in 5:11, "you must not associate with anyone who calls himself a brother but is sexually immoral or greedy, an idolater or a slanderer, a drunkard or a swindler. With such a man do not even eat." Paul is not advocating that only the sinless can

be members of the church; rather he is concerned about those who per-
sist in the very activities from which they have been freed through the
sacrifice of the Passover lamb (v 7). Are we to see Paul's lists of sins in
1Co 5 as an exhaustive list? Could we not add to Paul's list many more
sins? What about husbands who beat their wives, or wives who are
rebellious toward their husbands? Are marriages out of the jurisdiction
of church discipline?

Jay Adams, who has written numerous books on counseling and
church discipline, says, "Strangely, some never think of using church
discipline, even informal discipline, when the two parties are husband
and wife. Why not? A Christian husband and wife are not merely
married persons, they are also brother and sister in Christ's church. Most
marital problems could be resolved early by active, informal disciplin-
ary action" (*Handbook of Church Discipline*, 36).

In no place does Scripture delineate between those sins that warrant church discipline and those that don't. All sin is serious, and, if left
unchecked in a believer, could result in the Christian's spiritual demise.
Christians confronting one another, one-on-one, in love and humility,
is a normal part of a healthy, growing church. At this point someone
might ask the question, "Do I have to go to my brother about every little
offense?" The answer is no. Pr 10:12 says that love covers a multitude
of sins. Pr 19:11 says that to overlook an offense is a glorious thing. If
we had to bring up every annoyance between us we would probably
spend all our time doing so.

Any offense that does not come between us and the one who committed the offense does not need to be raised. However, if the offense
creates an unreconciled state between us and another the offense must
be brought up and dealt with. Any matter what makes you feel different
toward that person or hinders your ability to cover over the offense with
love must be dealt with. Of course, there are a few who take advantage
of the discipline process and spend an unnecessary amount of time confronting others. These individuals need to be taught the virtue of over-
looking an offense, and if they refuse to learn, they themselves may
become divisive and may need to be confronted by others.

Most church discipline cases will be settled in steps one or two
without advancing any further. However, there are times when the offender refuses to listen and thus forces the matter to steps three and four
(where the entire church enters the discipline process). By moving from
step two to step three the offender has displayed willful disobedience
and is now treading on serious ground. Now that the matter has come
before the church, what is the church's responsibility toward the of-

fender?

According to the Scriptures, the following requirements must be adhered to if biblical church discipline is to be properly administered:
1. "Special note" must be made of the offender (2Th 3:14). What Paul means is that the offender is to be identified to the whole church.
2. "Do not associate with him" (2Th 3:14; 1Co 5:11).
3. "Keep away" from him (2Th 3:6); Thayer's Greek-English Lexicon says, "to abstain from familiar intercourse with one."
4. "With such a man do not even eat." (1Co 5:11); eating with someone is a sign of fellowship.

It should be noted that these requirements given by the Apostle Paul are not just advice, but commands (2Th 3:6). During this third step of the discipline process, if the offender continues in willful disobedience, the church is to withdraw from him. That is, to disassociate from him in order that he may feel ashamed (2Th 3:14) and as a consequence come to repentance. The church is still to regard the offender "as a brother" (2Th 3:15), but as one whose status is in question. For fear that the offender may find justification for his rebellious actions, it is essential that every church member avoid normal fellowship with him. Any contact with the offender should consist of encouraging him to repent and obey the instructions of the church. Refusing fellowship is the very thing Paul is commanding in step three. This is not to be confused with step four, which is "removing from the midst," or "handing over to Satan." If the offender fails to heed the warning of the church he is to be removed from the church and handed over to Satan, "so that the flesh may be destroyed and his spirit saved on the day of the Lord" (1Co 5:5). The offender is no longer considered to be a believer, but must be treated "as a pagan and a tax collector" (Mt 18:17). While the church makes no final judgment as to the heart condition of the offender, it must judge his words and actions (1Co 5:12-13).

Church discipline is a blessing and a privilege provided by the Lord to aid in the restoration of sinning members. Sadly, in the church today, there are those who object to its practice. The following are some common objections that are often given in defense of not practicing church discipline.

•"Church discipline is not loving." God, who is Love, is the very One who commands that discipline be practiced in the church (Mt 18). Jesus, speaking to the church in Laodicea, says "Those whom I love I rebuke and discipline. So be earnest, and repent" (Re 3:19). If we are to imitate the love of Jesus we must care enough about our brothers to reprove them whenever they are caught in a sin (Ga 6:1-2).

•"To implement church discipline on someone would be judging them." Mt 7:1-5 is often cited for support of this objection. That Mt 7:1-5 is not an absolute statement forbidding all forms of judging is seen in 7:6. Jesus says, "Do not give dogs what is sacred; do not throw your pearls to pigs." In order for Christians to obey Jesus' command, they must make a decision (or a judgment) as to who qualifies as dogs and pigs. What Jesus does forbid in Mt 7:1-5 is hypocritical judging. There is a world of difference between the sinful act of hypocritical judging (Mt 7:1-5) and the restorative act of judging of which Paul speaks (1Co 5:3-5, 12-13).

•"Church discipline could cause divisions." Unity is of supreme value within the church. But unity at the expense of obedience is artificial unity at best. Today's church has become more concerned about not offending its tithing members than it has about obeying Christ's commands. Church discipline, properly administered, will strengthen the church and bring about biblical unity (Ep 4:13).

Christian Restoration is not only a biblical commandment but also a right and privilege of every member of the church, and therefore should not be withheld. Churches that refuse to follow God's program for church discipline can, in the end, expect to find themselves disciplined by God Himself (1Co 11:31-32).

— Bill Grimes and David Johnson

# 17
## CHURCH FAMILIES

Mal 4:4-6 foretells of God's family plan for Israel (and later the church). It shows what God expected of Israeli families – hearts turned toward each other. This turn of heart in family matters parallels the New Covenant change of heart in Jer 31 where God says He will put His law into our hearts. Four hundred years later, the angel who appeared to Zechariah and announced the birth of John the Baptist quoted Mal 4 to explain John's purpose and ministry. In Lk 1:13-17, the angel describes John as the one who will "turn many of the sons of Israel to the Lord their God" and as the one who will "turn the hearts of the fathers to their children and the disobedient to the wisdom of the righteous - to make ready a people prepared for the Lord". The angel's style and arrangement of these two descriptions make them corollaries. He arranged everything around v 17a so that the facts about John's ministry would be obvious. John, as the forerunner, preached the message of turning toward the Lord, which in turn would restore the hearts of fathers to the hearts of their children.

One of the good works accompanying salvation will be a change in family attitudes and actions. The father will practice godly headship of the family; the mother will be the submissive support her husband needs as he strains to obey the Lord. The children will obey their father and mother. The family will love each other, will be kind to one another, and will be best friends with each other. In short, the family will be the model of the Godhead and Christianity upon the earth.

Children are not left out of this equation. We don't just "do our best and hope that they turn out all right." Look at Lk 1:17 again. The angel quoted only part of Mal 4:6. He substituted "the attitude of the disobedient to that of the righteous" for "the hearts of the children to the fathers." The angel thus tells us what it means to have the "hearts of the children turned toward their fathers." The turning of the children's hearts (as expressed in Malachi) means that they will obey their parents (as expressed in Luke). When salvation genuinely reaches the parents, the children will eventually change from being disobedient to being righteous. This change, however, is not without great effort on the part of the parents. They will strive for godliness in their children. Part of the "turning" is repenting of the worldly way of rearing children. Parents who do strive for godliness in their children will be rewarded with their children's hearts turned toward them in obedience.

## Church Leadership

All this has great impact upon church leadership.  Both the elder and the deacon "must manage his own family well and see that his children obey him with proper respect" (1Ti 3:4; 5; 12) and have children who "believe and are not open to the charge of being wild and disobedient" (Tit 1:6).  Marriage and children are requirements for being an elder.  But that requirement does not hold true for the traveling apostle – neither Paul nor Timothy were married, and they are not called elders. The apostle Peter, on the other hand, was married and calls himself an elder in 1Pe 5:1-3.

The elder must have children whose hearts are turned toward their parents.  The elder who is too busy with his own or church concerns (as "good" as they may be) fails to understand the absolute priority of rearing his children in a way pleasing to God.  Indications are that he himself has not turned to the Lord if his own heart is not turned to his children (Lk 1:13-17).  Who else sees him twenty-four hours a day at his best and his worst?  If he does not live out his Christianity before his children, who is he to export it to others?

## Evangelism

You might think that with the above emphasis upon children, they ought to be the objects of the church's evangelistic efforts.  But who were the objects of the apostles' evangelism?  The book of Acts shows us that the apostles evangelized the heads of households, not children. Cornelius, Lydia, and the Philippian jailer all came to Christ because of the apostles' efforts.  Amazingly, their whole households came with them.  Is this only a cultural phenomena of that century?  I don't think so.  If we aim our evangelism at the fathers (or single mothers) we will, by the NT example, get the children.  The man whose heart truly turns to the Lord will turn toward his children, and they too will likely come to Christ.

## Church Discipline

Family matters relate directly to church discipline.  The man who follows God will discipline his children (Ep 6:4, NASB).  He will hold his children accountable for their actions and train them to obey him and his wife (see Pr 1:8; 2:1; 3:1; 4:1; 5:1; etc.).

Modern churches do not discipline the disobedient members because we have forgotten the biblical reasons and methods for disciplining our own children. As we have raised generations of children without biblical discipline, we have also raised the same generations to expect that no one can hold them accountable for their actions, least of all a church whose only requirements of them are their money and a few hours a week of their time. Children who have been raised to expect those in authority over them to provide needed discipline will not run from the church which seeks to discipline them for their good. In fact, children who have been raised in the discipline and instruction of the Lord will need very little church discipline as adults. We would be amazed at the transformation of our churches (and our society) over a generation if we would discipline our children to respond to God-given authority and not reject their father's discipline (Pr 3:11,12; and Heb 12:5-6) and, subsequently, the church's discipline.

## CHURCH MEETINGS

I am convinced that children of all ages should be with the parents in the house church meeting. If we take Ep 6:4 at face value, it is the father who is to train his children, not another adult teacher. The father who teaches his children the things of the Lord six days a week will not need someone else to do it on Sundays. A father who also disciplines his children will have them under control. His control will allow the children to be with the parents in the house church meeting. Remember that we are not training our children to remain children, but to be adults. They need to see how adults meet as a church and learn by participating as well. In our church, the families sit together. When necessary, the parents correct their children in our meetings or remove them for discipline, which some Sundays is often! But that is part of maturing as a church and as families. It is something we have taught and expect from our parents and children. Children can do far more than we sometimes require. If they need to nap, they sleep in Dad's or Mom's lap, or in the chair or on one of our beds. Often the children play with quiet toys, read, or color (sometimes on paper, and then sometimes on the floor!). It's just like family.

God's way of communicating truth to the next generation has not changed. God intends truth to be taught and learned by children in a family setting. Neither the church nor society has this direct responsibility; fathers and mothers do. The sooner we learn this lesson in the body of Christ, the sooner we will put aside all the worldly ways of teaching and training children and have generations of godly men and women in the church who can turn the world upside down once again.

## CHRISTIAN MINISTRY

Paul's concept of ministry was derived partially from family life. Paul drew upon a godly family as he illustrates his own apostolic ministry to the Thessalonians in 1Th 2:5-12. He used the nursing mother, and then the father, as examples. As an apostle, Paul could have been paid for his work among them as he preached the Gospel and taught them discipleship. However, he worked hard among them day and night so they would not think him greedy. A nursing mother who cares for her children day and night provided the perfect example of Paul's service. Her emotional ties to her children propel her in her ministry of love and devotion. She nurtures her children in contrast with the man's primary role. Women are to be the nurturer in the home, and their emphasis on relationships gives impetus to Paul's ministry. Paul's tender care, and his willingness to sacrifice his time and energy for their welfare, imitated the godly mother caring for her children.

On the other hand, Paul also looked to the godly father who was very concerned with the righteousness of his children and apparently, their reputation. Paul convincingly wrote that the father directing the moral development of the children proved to be the perfect example for the apostle exhorting, encouraging, and imploring the new Christians at Thessalonica to walk worthy of God. This goes back again to the father's responsibility to his children; teaching them righteousness and training them to that standard. However, the father who loves his children and wants God's blessing upon them does not impose legalism upon the household. That breeds rebellion. Christians do not earn a right standing before God, nor keep it, by what they do. It means that through the relationship we have with our children, we fathers urge as strongly as possible our children's obedient walk with God. Paul capitalized on his observations of godly men who concern themselves with their children's conduct.

The passive father will raise sons who are themselves passive and liable to be dominated by women. His daughters will tend to be domineering in all areas of family, church, and society. The emotionless mother will produce children who cannot relate to people. All this can be prevented by involved fathers and mothers who see to the well-being of their children and teach them the proper roles of men and women in the family, church, and society. It seems to me that Paul took the outstanding characteristics of the mother and father and applied them to his ministry: the emotional ties which caused sacrifice by the mother and the desire for children worthy of the family name which caused

168

much involvement by the father. We must do the same.

CONCLUSION

A church is a family. Paul names it the "household of God," calls salvation "adoption as sons," describes us as "heirs," tells Timothy to "entreat an elder as a father," calls Christians "brother" and "sister," and uses a childhood name for father (*abba*) to address the heavenly Father. All of these descriptions point to the relationships we have to God and to one another.

A family is people relating to one another. Church relationships, good and bad, overwhelm the NT reader if he looks for them. The good church nurtures and builds those relationships and does not substitute an endless parade of activities for them. People desire healthy relationships more than anything else. However, house church members must be prepared to get close, very close. Think of it as porcupines snuggling up to get warm in the winter. The closer they get, the more quills they feel. When they draw back, they get cold. It is better to feel the quills!

The house church model best resembles a family because it meets where people live. The family who hosts a church meeting and the members who go there draw themselves together as a unit. The atmosphere is real, not surreal. The conversation does not compete with the organ prelude, the relationships with the clothes and cars, or the truth with hypocrisy.

The church which meets in a home also best contributes to a family's spirituality and best enables a father as the head of the family to encourage their well-being. A house church allows the free time to teach one's family what it means to be a Christian in the kingdom of Christ and God. Indeed, it does not just allow; it places upon a father that responsibility because there is no one else designated to do it. One cannot delegate this duty to a Sunday School teacher, Bible study leader, youth minister, or minister – there are none of those in a house church. The weekly teaching does not substitute for the father's teaching, but complements it.

— Tim Melvin

*Tim teaches an excellent weekend seminar on biblical child training that I highly recommend. Contact him about coming to your church to present it! — Editor*

# GROWING PAINS:  GETTING TOO BIG

In the most common scriptural sense of the term, "the church" can never get too big.  As long as the Lord leaves His people on this earth, it will always be His intent for the church to grow.  And even in the sense of the true local church (all the truly redeemed ones in a locality) it is always God's intent for us to welcome growth as a blessing (try a Bible search on "multiply" for a sense of God's heart on numerical growth).

But what about a given congregation of saints meeting together regularly?  Is it possible for such a gathering to become too large?  In today's "church" paradigm, that hardly seems conceivable.  After all, the goal is numerical growth, isn't it?  Isn't growth evidence of spiritual health, of fulfilling the great commission?  The bigger a "church" is, the more effective it must be, right?  The more congregants in a "church," the more varied and specialized its programs can become, meeting more specific needs.  Such assumptions as these are common, but do they really reflect God's desire for His house?

The growing number of Christians involved with house churches sense a longing for intimacy in fellowship with other believers around the Lord.  And many have experienced the increasingly impersonal characteristics of program-centered "churches," especially as they become larger (or endeavor to seem larger than they are).  Many have sensed the disconnect of being disenfranchised by the increasingly professional production that many churches aspire to provide in their "services."

"As for me and my house," I find compelling the scriptural arguments favoring churches meeting exclusively in private homes.  Paul's insistence (1Co 4:16-17; 11:1-2, 16; 14:33; Ep 2:20; Php. 3:17; 4:9; 2Th 2:15; 3:6-9; 1Ti 1:16; 1Ti 3:14-15; 2Ti 1:13)  that the churches follow the apostolic "pattern" (and his own example) are persuasive arguments against the notion that where churches meet is not a matter of scriptural mandate.

Gathering around the Lord in an authentic way is so exciting, interesting, and enjoyable that numerical growth will likely result, in time, as saints mature corporately in their proficiency in letting the Holy Spirit lead their feasts/gatherings. So what should churches do when they grow to the point that they can no longer fit in a typical private home?  How many is too big?

Jesus used an analogy (a parable - Mt 9:17; Mk 2:22; Lk 5:37-39) contrasting new and old wine and wineskins in defending His disciples' lack of fasting. Clearly the wine is more important than the wineskin, but the wrong wineskin can be detrimental to the benefit of the wine. The function is more important than the form, but the wrong form can inhibit the intended function.

It is always risky (and thus sometimes questionable) to speculate on God's purposes for His acts. Yet He calls us to learn His ways (Ps 25:4; 51:13; 95:10). Let me cautiously ponder why the New Testament church was so consistently portrayed as gathering in homes. I suspect a key is to be found in Paul's explicit description of a church gathering in which "all things [are] done decently and in order" (1Co 14:40).

Throughout 1Co 14, Paul contrasts practices that are disorderly and confusing with those that orderly and edifying. Interestingly, Paul's definition of orderliness is significantly different from what many of us would find comfortable, at least in a formal meeting (which may be a key to understanding the problem). Paul cautions against such confusing practices as speaking out in languages other people don't understand, having more than one person speaking at a time, having women lead, and other things focusing on one's own enjoyment rather than the benefit of the whole group. But then he contrasts these with descriptions of orderly, edifying corporate experiences.

For example, after portraying an inappropriate situation in which "an unbeliever or uninformed person" (presumably an uninformed believer) comes in where "the whole church comes together in one place, and all speak in tongues" and concludes "that you are all out of your mind" (1Co 14:23), Paul then describes the appropriate alternative. Interestingly, the better practice is not sitting still and listening to experts expound on scripture. Instead, Paul says (1Co 14:24-25) that "if *all* prophesy," this "unbeliever or uninformed person" will be "convinced by *all*" and "judged by *all.*" The final outcome is that "falling on his face [this is orderly?] he will worship God and report that God is truly among you."

The incredible thing is that this prophetic participation by "all" is what Paul means by "decently and in order." He goes on to argue (verse 26) that when the brothers come together "each one" brings something to "be done for edification." These things might include "a psalm," "a teaching," "a tongue," "a revelation," or "an interpretation." Note that this list includes things that could be planned ahead, but also things that couldn't likely be previously prepared.

## Chapter 18:  Growing Pains:  Getting Too Big

A little later he says (verse 30) that if someone is speaking and "anything is revealed to another who sits by," the first speaker is to welcome the interruption and let the second brother speak.  He continues with the phenomenal contention (verse 31) that "you can *all* prophesy one by one."  At first glance this seems to contradict his directive two verses earlier to "Let two or three prophets speak and let the others judge."  If only two or three can prophesy, yet he says "all" can prophesy, one possible interpretation is that there should only be two or three brothers present.  Although I doubt this is the correct interpretation of the passage, it would certainly point to relatively small gatherings.

Actually, I suspect the correct interpretation is that the prophecies were to be voiced conversationally, among two or three brothers, with those listening in discerning whether or not they are hearing the voice of the Shepherd (Jn 10:3-5, 16, 27).  This still sounds like a fairly intimate conversation, with some participating and the others leaning forward (inclining their hearts) as they listen with their ears and their spirits.

Even in the next section, where Paul addresses the women's dynamic silence (exerting unspoken pressure on the men to lead out), there is a sense of the interactive context of the gathering when he says (verse 35), "if they want to learn something, let them ask their own husbands at home."  Apparently the men were to be free to interact during the gathering, asking questions.  It is clear that the church gathering envisioned by the apostle was interactively participatory, personally intimate, and spontaneously led by the Holy Spirit, yet orderly in the sense that each person was to consider the good of the group rather than simply his own edification (considerate).  A congregation is too large if "all" cannot participate intimately.

An interesting thing about private homes is that they are seldom large enough to facilitate gatherings of more than just a few families.  I think we are wise, and cooperating with the Lord's ways, when we choose to design our homes to facilitate groups of saints to meet there.  But is it possible the Lord ordained that churches gather house to house in order to keep the numbers relatively small?  If so, we might be undermining His intent when we seek for larger facilities.

If I could build a house with a living room that could facilitate gatherings of 200 people, would that be an aide to the church?  Or might I possibly be compromising the Lord's design to keep groups somewhat smaller?  I doubt the Lord is pleased to have us set numerical limits.  Yet it appears to me there is a general principle we should anticipate regarding the size of congregations gathering together intimately.

In 1993, for the fourth time, our family began meeting together with a couple of other families as a "church." Over the years the size of the group has grown, and sometimes diminished. At one point some of us felt we had reached a size that was too large for a home. I suggested that we consider finding some larger hall in which to meet, but the Lord used several of the other brothers to keep us from going down that path. It appears the Lord's provision for us at that time was to have the size of the group diminish. Over a relatively short period of time several of the families moved to other regions, thus relieving the pressure of dealing with the question of what to do if the congregation becomes too numerous to fit in a home.

Recently the Lord has once again brought growth to the circle of saints we're walking among. There are currently five participating families living in our community of Springfield, California, whose geographic proximity allows a frequency of contact encouraging us to walk together in relative intimacy (although we all recognize a longing for the Lord to work more in bonding our hearts together around Him). Two other families are currently in the process of moving here. Another two families living about a half-hour away have expressed a desire (and realistic intentions) to move here. Two other participating families live within a half hour of Springville, and another two families live nearly an hour and two hours away, but have attended the weekly meetings for years. Finally, there are several other families who visit the weekly gatherings fairly often. (Those living further away are hindered from much of the "exhorting one another daily" experience of Heb 3:13, as a result of geographic limitations.)

We clearly are at a point where not all who want to gather with us can participate in a single meeting in a private home. If all the families who have identified as part of the congregation were present in one place, at one time, there would be ninety people. If any of the regular or infrequent visitors were present, that would be even more.

We want to hear the Lord's direction regarding what we should do regarding this situation. We could try to plan a response, but the likelihood of resolving on an approach that He doesn't find pleasure in is very high. Solomon said (twice, Pr 14:12 & 16:25), "There is a way that seems right to a man, But its end is the way of death." Yet the Lord is apparently pleased to have us ponder His ways revealed in scripture, and anticipate what He will likely lead. Let's consider some possible approaches, that might (or might not) eventually be what the Lord leads.

Although I seriously doubt the Lord would have us find a larger meeting place to accommodate everyone, that is a possibility that others have felt is pleasing to the Lord. It is certainly a possibility, though a doubtful one.

We could simply do nothing. This could be of the Lord as we "Stand still and see the salvation of the LORD" (2Ch 20:17). It's quite possible the Lord would provide a solution without asking any of us to change what we have been doing at all. Or He might call us to bear the crowding with joy. Most of us have heard stories of congregations in third world countries where lots of folks gather in a very confined space. But as things are now, few of the families are willing to open their homes for gatherings, knowing there is no way everyone will fit. It seems to me the incentive to avoid hospitality is something we should seek the Lord to eliminate.

Another possibility (however remote) is that the Lord would lead us to limit the number of folks who are welcome to gather with us. We could do as some homeschool support groups do and simply have a closed group, requiring any others who are interested in walking in the way the Lord is leading us, to find others to gather with. As doubtful as this option is to me, I want to leave the door open to whatever the Lord leads.

An option that has been discussed among many in the "house church" movement is the obvious possibility of multiplying by splitting a large group in two. This could be done based on geography, or it could be done based on some other method (casting lots, number or ages of family members, common interests, convictions, theology, etc.). It seems to me that distinguishing one church from another on the basis of anything other than geography is the kind of factiousness that Paul addressed in the first several chapters of 1 Corinthians. Choosing to fellowship only with folks who are similar to myself is a tacit acceptance of divisions in the body. If I must conclude that someone is truly a member of the body of Christ, I must also welcome fellowship with that person.

A couple of the families we gather with, who live quite a ways from many of the rest of us, have expressed fear that they might sometime be asked to split off and form a distinct group. Interestingly, if all the non-Springville families were to gather together, distinct from the Springville families (including those definitely moving here), the two groups would have exactly the same number of families. This is certainly a possibility the Lord could lead. However, my sense is that such an arbitrary division smacks of human manipulation rather than listening to the leading of the Holy Spirit.

Yet in scripture geographic distinctions in the church were the one legitimate basis for unique church identity. The church in Antioch was one with the church in Jerusalem, but there was a sense in which they were distinct churches. There is only one body of Christ, made up of all believers of all time throughout the world. But there are distinct churches (plural) based on geography (not on human loyalties, distinctive practices, or unique theological positions). While we must admit that the modern church is splintered, the solution is to see the church from Jesus' perspective. There is thus only one church in Springville, California, and all the Christians in Springville are part of the church in Springville. Even all the Christians in the church of Springville can't possibly (and, I believe, shouldn't) meet regularly in one place. If we don't meet in one place because there are too many of us, how do we decided who meets where?

Another possibility is scheduling meetings at different times, and welcoming folks participating in the meetings that best fit their schedule and preferences. Certainly this is an approach that is considered a "no-brainer" for institutional "churches" that outgrow their "sanctuary." We could have an "early service" and a "late service." (I'm almost gagging as I write this.) Folks could choose which love feast they want to participate in. They might alternate participation, and even occasionally enjoy both feasts. Perhaps several of the brothers who sense a special calling to provide oversight to the congregation could particularly make it a point to participate in both groups.

These are exciting times, as we find the Lord leading us in paths that are distinct from the traditions that have been set over the centuries. May we humble ourselves before the Lord, acknowledging that we can't figure out the best approaches, and are utterly dependent upon the Holy Spirit's leading, in order to truly be a pleasure to our Bridegroom.

— Jonathan Lindvall

# 19

# CHURCH TRADITIONS

It is amazing to realize, though nevertheless simply a fact, that Jesus' conflict with Israel, and in particular with Israel's religious leaders, was not over the Mosaic Law. Jesus kept the Old Covenant to the letter. Apart from one rather embarrassing attempt to trip Him up using the occasion of a woman being caught in adultery, those who sought to do battle against Him did so for entirely other reasons. What made them so mad with Jesus wasn't that He went against anything in the Old Testament scriptures (He patently didn't) but rather that He challenged and broke something called the *tradition of the elders*. We therefore read in Mark's Gospel, "Now when the Pharisees and some of the scribes who had come from Jerusalem gathered around him, they noticed that some of his disciples were eating with defiled hands, that is, without washing them. (For the Pharisees, and all the Jews, do not eat unless they thoroughly wash their hands, thus observing the tradition of the elders; and they do not eat anything from the market unless they wash it; and there are also many other traditions that they observe, the washing of cups, pots, and bronze kettles.) So the Pharisees and the scribes asked him, 'Why do your disciples not live according to the tradition of the elders, but eat with defiled hands?'" (Mk 7:1-5). So what, precisely, is going on here? The answer is that whereas in theory Israel considered the Old Testament scriptures to be it's final authority in matters of both faith and practice, the reality was somewhat different. The Jews actually paid far more heed to a system of teaching and practice known variously as the tradition of the elders, or the Oral Law.

Pharisaic Judaism taught that when Moses was on Mount Sinai he was given not one, but two sets of laws by God; the written law, or Mosaic Law, which was recorded in the pages of the Old Testament, and also a second secret law that was passed on purely orally down through the generations, and which came to public light in the years preceding the time of Jesus. Of course when the inevitable conflict between these two laws, and what they taught, came about, Israel had to eventually decide which one was their actual final authority. After all, you may claim to have two things as your equal final authority, here the Old Testament and the Oral Law, but you really only have one, and it is that which you obey once the contradictions between the two emerge. Incredibly, Israel went with the Oral Law, the tradition of the elders, and relegated the Mosaic Law, and their Old Testament scriptures, to second place. Indeed, the Pharisees taught, and quite unashamedly too, that it was more punishable to act against the tradition of the elders than it was the Old Testament scriptures.

What we must therefore understand is that at the time of Jesus the nation of Israel lived under the authority of a system of teachings and practices which, in numerous vitally important ways, went completely against teachings and practices laid down in the Old Testament: yet they did so whilst claiming to have been led to do so by God Himself under the pretext that this Oral Law had supposedly been given to Moses by Him. A system of completely man-made and merely humanly originated teachings and practices had therefore usurped and replaced the revealed truth of the written Word of God, yet with the claim that such traditions and teachings had come from the Lord God of Israel Himself, even though they contradicted the Old Testament scriptures. However, if we ask what the Lord God of Israel thought about this supposedly inspired Oral Law, then all we have to do is to look at Jesus' responses to it. He said to them, "Isaiah prophesied rightly about you hypocrites, as it is written, 'This people honours me with their lips, but their hearts are far from me; in vain do they worship me, teaching human precepts as doctrines.' You abandon the commandment of God and hold to human tradition" (Mk 7:6-8).

Hypocrisy! That was the Lord's clear and unwavering verdict on traditions which cause His people to go against the inspired traditions as revealed in the Word of God. To hold to merely humanly originated practice, whatever it may be, as opposed to biblical practice is, according to the Lord Jesus Christ, to "abandon the commandment of God".

I think you'll agree that this is heavy duty stuff, and I can imagine the kind of responses even now being elicited from my readers: "Amen brother! That's terrible what Israel did!" "Imagine that: Israel going against the Mosaic Law in favour of their own man made teachings and practices and traditions. No wonder God judged them!" "What? Abandoning the commandment of God by holding to merely human tradition? Unthinkable!" But I have to tell you that, for virtually two millennia, we Christians have been doing exactly the same thing.

It is incredible beyond words to realize, though nevertheless also simply a fact, that when it comes to our experience of church life, by which I mean the traditions, or established practice, which the vast majority of Christians unquestioningly follow and implement, virtually all of it is based on a system of teachings and practices which, just like Israel's tradition of the elders, has nothing whatsoever to do with the

Word of God. Far from being what we see revealed in the pages of the New Testament, it rather originated from, and was implemented by, men who came on the scene after the Apostles of Jesus were dead, and therefore after the writing of the New Testament was completed.

What we must grasp here is that these traditions are not just different from what we see in scripture in the sense of merely being variations, they actually equate to being the complete opposite of what we see in the New Testament. Far from being mere developments whereby biblical practices are applied in slightly different ways in differing circumstances and conditions, they are rather practices which are at complete variance with what is taught in the New Testament, and which go against it in virtually every possible respect. They are teachings and practices that, without any doubt whatsoever, cause those adhering to them to go completely and directly against what we see revealed in the Word of God, the very thing Jesus so blatantly and unwaveringly condemned.

I am going to make some observations now which no Bible commentator, scholar or historian worth his salt would challenge. They pertain to the way in which churches in New Testament times were set up and organized according to the teachings and traditions passed on by the Apostles of Jesus and as revealed in their writings, the very New Testament itself. And I am simply going to describe what it was like when a group of believers met together as a church as revealed in the pages of scripture: and let me emphasize too, revealed so clearly that, as I have already mentioned, no scholar would in any way challenge it.

So let's go back in time to the midway point of the first century and see what church was like in New Testament times. And the immediate thing to say is that when you went to the coming together of the particular church you were part of you would have found yourself, without fail, going to someone's house. Numbers would therefore be small, and you would be part of as intimate number of people who knew you, and who you knew, very well. *Extended family* would be the idea that best described it, and the general tenor of the gathering would have been, at all points, that of intimate informality. When you thus came together with your brothers and sisters two things would have happened.

Firstly, though this is not meant to imply any set chronological order, there would be a time of sharing together during which all were free to take part as they felt the Lord was leading them to. From worshipful singing, to prayer and intercession, from bringing a teaching, to declaring a prophesy, from sharing a burden to speaking a word of knowledge or wisdom, all would be free to take part. No one led the proceedings from the front in any way: indeed, being in someone's

179

lounge, and with everyone sitting face to face around the room as opposed to being in rows merely looking at the back of someone's neck, there is no *front* to lead from. All is spontaneous, free, unstructured and Spirit-led nature. The atmosphere is that of worshipful, reverent and casual joy.

Then secondly, everyone present would have eaten a meal together. In fact, you would together eat your main meal of the day. And part of this meal would have been a loaf of bread and a cup of wine that all shared in common, this reminding the assembled church that Jesus is the guest of honor and that, though an ordinary shared meal, this was also a very special shared meal - the Lord's Supper and Table. This, the covenant meal of individual believers gathered as a corporate church, would have been what bound you all together as an extended family of God in whatever area you were located.

There is something else you would most likely notice too, and it is that any leadership, such as existed, is very, very low-key indeed, and far more of a *back seat* affair than anything *up front*. Further, any such leadership would be seen purely as a functional matter, and would in no way be thought of as being a positional with official titles or the like. Moreover, it would also have been plural, and any idea of one man being in charge would have been foreign thought indeed to those gathered. Something else these men (for leaders were always men in the New Testament churches) would have had in common was that they all originated from that same church and were home grown guys, local lads who everyone in the church knew extremely well. As for names (there were no official titles) they were variously called elders, overseers or bishops (depending on which translation of the Bible you read) and pastors or shepherds (again, depending on translation), with each being synonymous terms for the same group of men. Those with various other ministries (apostles, prophets, teachers etc) might sometimes pass through in order to help out here and there as invited, but they would eventually move on to other places and the only ongoing leadership in the church would have been these local and home grown older brothers. They ensured that the format was always that of open and spontaneous free participation, and *leading from the front* was the last thing they wanted to do, and for the simple reason that they had been taught by the Apostles that such was not the Lord's intention for them.

And that is what church gatherings were like whilst the teachings and traditions of the Apostles, as revealed to us in the New Testament, held sway. Further, and do please underline this in red ink, I repeat what I earlier said that no Bible commentator, scholar or historian worth his salt would question my description in any significant way. I have simply laid out what is there, as simple matters of fact, in the pages of the New Testament. We find in scripture only one prescribed way in which believers were taught to come together as churches and to do things - so how do we do things today when we come together as churches? In fact, how have believers been doing it for pretty much the whole of church history? As I pointed out earlier, we don't just do things differently, we do them virtually exactly the opposite!

For a start, we meet in large numbers in public buildings. Let me ask: Is that merely a variation on meeting in small numbers in private homes? No, it is the exact opposite!

Secondly, we have *services* which are led from the front by (usually) professional paid leaders, which positively ensures that all are not free to partake as the Spirit leads and as scripture teaches. Tell me, is that merely a variation on an open and completely participatory gathering without leadership from the front and with all free to take part? No, it is the exact opposite!

Thirdly, after the main *service* (and we have just seen that the New Testament churches didn't have anything that even vaguely resembled *worship services*) we tack on another one, a ritual with bread and wine. Again I ask, is that merely a variation on having a meal together? No, it's a totally different thing altogether! It is something that would have been completely alien to the Apostles who rather taught the churches to share a meal together; indeed, the very Lord's Supper! (The Greek word employed in scripture, *deipnon*, means the main meal of the day towards evening.)

Lastly, though there are other things I could have included, but space doesn't allow, how do we go about leadership? What does it look like in our churches as opposed to the churches back then? Well, we bring in hierarchical and positional leadership from the outside in the shape of an individual with an official title of some kind. That is, we usually go for variations on the theme of having one man at the top, and virtually always a paid professional brought in from the outside as well. Compare that with non-positional, plural, home-grown brothers who aren't professionally salaried, and I again ask: Is that merely a variation of some kind? Is it just tinkering at the edges and just moving things round a little? No, it is the complete opposite of the way the church did things as taught by the Apostles of Jesus. (And where did they get their ideas from? From the Lord Himself!)

We must be aware too that it is irrelevant as to which church we are talking about here. Whether Orthodox, Catholic or Presbyterian, whether Anglican or Baptist, whether Pentecostal or Methodist, whether Episcopalian or Free Evangelical, when it comes to church practice all are similarly based on the same traditions and teachings of men who appeared after the canon of scripture was closed, and who taught practices that go against the revealed Word of God. (All the aforementioned churches are based in buildings, with religious *services* and bread and wine rituals, and all likewise practice leadership that flies in the face of what we see revealed in scripture.)

The Early Church Fathers, as history has named the men who took on the leadership of the Christian churches in the years and generations after the Apostles died, did much good; but in the things we are looking at here they erred badly. And I am asking that we reject and renounce the false teachings and practices which they introduced (though not the biblically sound things they did and taught), and that we reject too the heritage of the completely unbiblical church life and experience they have subsequently bequeathed to us. As I have already made clear, no one who knows their biblical stuff would challenge how I have described New Testament church life and practice in contrast to the way in which the Fathers changed things; but what I, and many others, are saying, and here is where the debate rages, is that they were wrong to teach what they taught, and that we have likewise been wrong through the centuries to have continued with it all.

Israel disobeyed the Old Testament at various points because of their beloved, yet totally wrong and unbiblical, tradition of the elders. The Christian Church has done exactly the same thing, only with the tradition of the Early Church Fathers and New Testament revelation. In England we call that a double-whammy, and it's time to start putting it right. The traditions of death, or the traditions of the Divine? I leave you, dear reader, to decide for yourself!

— Beresford Job

*For a fully documented presentation on the tradition of the Jewish elders and its parallel with the tradtions of the Early Church Fathers, request the Traditions tape series, by Beresford Job, from www.ntrf.org. For corroboration from biblical scholars concerning what the New Testament churches were like, visit the Chigwell Christian Fellowship website at www.house-church.org. — Editor*

# 20
## CONCLUSION

Throughout history, God has raised up men to call the church to obedience, action, or accountability. Such men have often found themselves in the age-old struggle of whether to remain within the system and attempt to rebuild the church from within (as Puritans), or whether to leave it and follow the Lord in unfettered obedience (as Separatists). Good men have taken both approaches.

During the 1500s there were two church reformations going on simultaneously. The more famous Protestant reformation was headed by such men as Martin Luther and John Calvin. (Though Luther began as a Puritan, he was forced into Separatism when the Catholic Church excommunicated him.) These Protestant reformers helped restore the theology (orthodoxy) of the church to such Biblical teachings as salvation by grace through faith. To them we are deeply indebted.

However, the reformers did not completely rebuild church practice (orthopraxy). Just as Constantine (a fourth century "Christian" Roman emperor) had turned pagan temples into Christian cathedrals, the Protestants largely just turned Catholic cathedrals into Protestant ones. Less famous (and to some, more infamous) was the so-called Radical reformation. These reformers also desired to see God's church restored to its NT origins, not just in its theology, but even in its practice. They were called "radical" by their persecutors, "radical" in the sense of being "extreme" or even unbalanced. Their persecutors, sadly, were both the Catholics and the Protestants (which, based on Jn 13:34-35, qualifies them as somewhat "infamous" themselves). But just how balanced were some of God's greatest servants? How balanced was Jeremiah, who went around continually wailing? What of Ezekiel, who laid down on his left side for over a year, and then turned over to his right side for forty days? And then there was Isaiah, who went naked for three years. Do these men sound balanced to you? When it comes to obeying Scripture, "radical" is what the Lord expects!

As the unbelieving Jewish establishment persecuted the early church, as the Catholics persecuted the Protestants, as both Catholics and Protestants persecuted the Anabaptists, and as the Anglicans persecuted the Baptists, so too you can expect at least some degree of opposition when you opt to take a stand for Truth. Be glad and rejoice! Great will be your reward in heaven (Mt 5:12).

The journey before you may well be a difficult one. Disillusionment, loneliness, discouragement, and disappointment potentially lie in wait. In such times, remember to look to the Lord to work His power through your weakness. Besides, it is *His* church anyway and ultimately *His* problem. Jesus isn't worried about anything!

In order to have any real hope for success in achieving NT church life, at least two things are necessary from the core group. First, there must be an absolute, resolute, unshakable love for Jesus that is expressed an absolute, resolute, unshakable commitment to obey all His commands. Thus, God's Word must be held up as the inerrant authority governing all that is said, thought, or done. Second, the core group must possess an undying love for the brethren. Unless there is a total commitment to both the Lord and His people, any house church is in serious trouble (cp Jn 14:15, 21-24 15:9-17).

We must love Jesus enough to bring our churches into compliance with everything Jesus commanded. We must also love the brethren enough to put up with their faults, shortcomings, and shortsightedness. People do have problems. No one is perfect. Thus, rebuilders must be patient, long suffering, and understanding of others in the fellowship.

As it turns out, "extreme" is not the only meaning of "radical." It is from the Latin *radix* and simply means "root." The Radical reformers wanted to go back, past Constantine, all the way to the church's NT roots. Let's join in and help complete all that was good about both reformations. After the Judeans had been in Babylonian captivity for seventy years, God providentially raised up a pagan ruler who was inclined to grant the Jews freedom to return home to their Promised Land. Few, however, found it convenient to return home. Babylon was just too comfortable and Jerusalem too devastated. Only a minority, led by Nehemiah, Ezra, and Zerubbabel, ventured forth to rebuild that which had been lost. A similar choice is facing you. Regardless of whether you opt to be a Puritan or a Separatist, will you help rebuild the church, or will you remain at ease in Babylon?

— Steve Atkerson

# ABOUT THE AUTHORS

**BRIAN ANDERSON** — Brian and his wife Debbie live in Sonora, California and have two grown sons. Brian was the full-time pastor of a Bible church before becoming involved with biblical house churches. He is now a bi-vocational house church planter. He also plays the five-string banjo in a bluegrass band and often finds opportunities through this venue to proclaim the gospel. Brian has many of his teachings posted at WWW.SOLIDROCK.NET.

**STEVE ATKERSON** — Steve and his wife Sandra live in Atlanta and homeschool their three children. Steve earned an M.Div. from Mid America Baptist Theological Seminary and then served seven years as one of the pastors of a Southern Baptist Church. He resigned in 1990 to work with biblical house churches. Steve is now a bi-voational local house church elder, itinerant teacher, and president of the *New Testament Restoration Foundation*. He can be contacted through WWW.NTRF.ORG.

**BILL GRIMES** — Bill, Ruth and their daughter Mary Catherine live in Lawrenceville, Georgia. Bill has a master's degree from Reformed Theological Seminary in Jackson, Mississippi and was involved with Christian education before returning to secular employment. He has been home churching since 1990.

**BERESFORD JOB** — Beresford is a full time house church elder near London, England. He is married to Belinda and they have a daughter, Bethany. Beresford was born-again in 1971 and was soon conducting an evangelistic ministry. However, he eventually moved into a much less itinerant pastoral and teaching function and was recognized as an elder at the Chigwell Christian Fellowship when it began in 1988. Their church web site is WWW.HOUSE-CHURCH.ORG.

**DAVID JOHNSON** — David and his wife Molly have four home schooled children. David has been participating in house churches since 1992 and is a bi-vocational elder at a church in Atlanta. David holds to the Doctrines of Grace and New Covanant Theology. His business site is: WWW.CLEARVIEWWINDOWCLEANING.COM

**JONATHAN LINDVALL** — Jonathan and his wife, Connie, have homeschooled their six children from birth. Their family is part of house church in Springville, California. Jonathan is the administrator of a local homeschool ministry, and president of Bold Christian Living, conducting the BOLD PARENTING Seminar, the BOLD CHRISTIAN YOUTH Seminar, House Church Seminars, and other workshops. He comes from a wide background in public and private education, pastoral ministry, and broadcasting. He earned his B.A. in Bible/Theology and Social Science from Bethany Bible College, Santa Cruz, California, and M.A. in Educational Administration from California State University, Bakersfield. He can be contacted through his web site: WWW.BOLDCHRISTIANLIVING.COM.

**TIM MELVIN** — After college, a short stint as a remodeling contractor, and a military career, Tim earned an M.Div. degree from Mid-America Baptist Theological Seminary while serving on several church staffs in Memphis. He then did three years of doctoral work in Hebrew and Old Testament while teaching Research,Writing, and English at MABTS. Once convinced of house church theology, Tim started several house churches in Memphis, Tennessee. He now manages a distribution center in Memphis. He and his wife Sarah reside in Olive Branch, Mississippi and have three grown daughters whom they home-educated for twelve years.

**HAL MILLER** — Hal has several theological degrees: a master's from Gordon-Conwell and a doctorate in systematic theology from Boston College. Formerly an ethics professor, he now earns his living in the secular sector and has spent over twenty-five years in a network of house churches in Salem, Massachusetts. Hal and his family now live in Virginia. He has been instrumental in the development of the House Church Discussion List internet group, which may be accessed at WWW.GROUPS.YAHOO.COM/GROUP/HCDL/

**DAN TROTTER** — Dan and his wife Linda reside in rural South Carolina and have three grown children. He is an elder at a house church he helped plant in 1992 in the rural area where he lives. Dan has a Master's Degree in Church History from Trinity Evangelical Divinity School near Chicago, has been a lawyer, and is now a retired professor of business administration at Coker College in Hartsville, SC. His ministry is traveling and teaching on New Testament church life. He may be reached through his ministry's web site, *The New Reformation Review:* WWW.GEOCITIES.COM/ DANTROTTER.

**JON ZENS** — Jon has been the editor of Searching Together, a quarterly magazine, since 1978, runs the Searching Together Bookstore in Taylors Falls, MN, and is one of the elders of a house church on the Minnesota/Wisconsin border. He received his theological training at Covenant College (1968), Westminster Theological Seminary (1972) and the California Graduate School of Theology.(1983), and has pastored several Baptist churches. Jon and his wife Dotty have three grown children and four grandchildren. He may be contacted through his web site: WWW.SEARCHINGTOGETHER.ORG.

•Banks, Robert and Julia. *The Church Comes Home*. Peabody, MA: Hendrickson Publishers, 1998

•*Bold Christian Living*. Jonathan Lindvall's ministry of home schooling, biblical parenting, and biblical home churching. www.boldchristianliving.com

•*Chigwell Christian Fellowship*. English Church web site with many articles by Beresford Job on church tradition versus apostolic tradition. www.house-church.org

•Delashmut, Gary, *Challenges to Christian Community*, cassette tapes t08746a & t08746b. 800-698-7884. www.xenos.org

•Dagg, JL, *Manual of Church Order* (Harrisonburg, VA: Gano Books, 1990)

•Erkel, Darryl. *Passive in the Pews*. Available from the author at: www.churchinfocus.org

•*Global Opportunities For Christ*. Bob Emery's ministry of providing support to indigenous third world evangelists and church planters. www.goforchrist.org

•*International Council on Inerrancy*. Classic statement drawn up in 1978 by leading evangelical scholars to combat downgraded liberal and neo-orthodox views of inspiration. www.churchcouncil.org

•Nee, Watchman. *The Normal Christian Church Life*. Available online at www.flash.net/~paidion/nee.htm

•*New Covenant Theology* web site: www.ids.org

•*New Reformation Review.* Dan Trotter's biblical church web site on Christ-centered, biblical, apostolic church life. www.geocities.com/dantrotter

•*Patriarch Magazine*, Phil Lancaster's ministry focusing on encouraging men to be the heads of their households. www.patriarch

•*Persecuted Church Collection.* Jon Dee's ministry of encouraging and financially supporting persecuted believers in China who have lost everything for the sake of the gospel.
www.persecutedchurch.com

•Piper & Grudem, *Recovering Biblical Manhood & Womanhood* (Wheaton, IL: Crossway Books, 1991). www.cbmw.org. Also of note: www.ladiesagainstfeminism.com

•*Searching Together.* Jon Zen's magazine exploring the "one another" aspect of church life in Jesus. P.O. Box 538, Saint Croix Falls, WI 54024. www.searchingtogether.org

•Snyder, Howard. *Radical Renewal: The Problem of Wineskins Today.* Houston: Touch, 1996

• Svendsen, Eric, *The Table of The Lord.* A scholarly presentation of the fact that the pristine church celebrated the Lord's Supper as a fellowship meal each week. Order from www.ntrmin.org

• VerDuin, Leonard. *The Reformers And Their Stepchildren.* Sarasota: Christian Hymnary, 1991. Order from www.searchingtogether.org

•*Vision Forum.* Douglas W. Phillips' ministry of uniting church and home. www.visionforum.com

# ABOUT NTRF

The New Testament Restoration Foundation is part of a growing body of believers who have come to see the importance of following New Testament church patterns. We have taken to heart the evangelical belief that the Bible is our final authority, not only in matters of faith, but also in matters of practice. We see theological significance in the distinctive traditions of the apostolic church.

The word "restoration" in our name does not reflect a belief on our part that the true church somehow ceased to exist after the time of the apostles. God has guided and preserved His elect throughout the years. We are deeply indebted to those who have gone before us and thankfully stand on their shoulders. The idea of "restoration" comes from our desire to see New Testament practices (ortho*praxy*) restored to today's church, just as New Testament theology (ortho*doxy*) was restored during the Reformation.

We seek to aid others in recapturing the intimacy, simplicity, acountability and dynamic of the first century church. Our goal is to provide, free of charge, resources and training in how the early church met together in community. Of course this does not mean the Foundation runs on air. Although we do not charge a fee, we do appreciate the generosity of those inclined to help underwrite our expenses. There is never any pressure or arm-twisting.

Those who are associated with the Foundation believe in the Doctrines of Grace, New Covenant Theology, and agree with the Chicago Statement on Biblical Inerrancy. The essential tenants of the faith to which we subscribe are identical to those found in the doctrinal statements of any sound evangelical institution. Our of our favorite statement of faith is the First London (Baptist) Confession of 1644 (also available from NTRF).

# NTRF PUBLICATIONS

Our desire is to provide, free of charge, resources and training in how the early church met together in community. In order to better allocate our resources, we generally only send out one item at a time. If, after digesting it, you still desire other of our materials, that will be gladly sent also! Please be sure to clearly state in your second request that you have already worked through the first material sent. Note that on a second or subsequent order, we will need your entire mailing address again. Please send all requests through our web site, WWW.NTRF.ORG.

• *Ekklesia . . . To The Roots Of Biblical Church Life* — An introductory book covering most topics related to New Testament church life: the Lord's Supper as a full meal, interactive meetings, consensus government, home-based churches, the importance of following NT patterns, the ministry of elders, full-time workers, integrating church and family, church discipline, giving, etc. (It replaces *Toward A House Church Theology*, now out of print).

• *Radio Talk Show Broadcast: House Churches* — A cassette recording of a radio call-in talk show about Biblical house churches. Great for introducing other believers to NT church life!

• *Searching for the New Testament Church* — A six tape audio cassette series that is both practical and theological in dealing with the main issues of New Testament church life (apostolic tradition, church government, church meetings, the Lord's Supper, house churches). A good resource for listening to while driving.

• *The Practice of The Early Church: A Theological Workbook* — A in-depth teacher's resource designed to help you lead a series of interactive discussions on what the Bible says about our Lord's church. Covers many of the same topics as are found in our book, *Ekklesia . . . To The Roots Of Biblical Church Life,* plus much more (sisters in service, baptism, the Lord's Day, etc.).

## Ekklesia . . . To The Roots of Biblical Church Life

• *Equipping Manual* — A one year study course designed to help equip believers for effective service. It covers Christian basics: how to study the Bible, salvation, evangelism, the origin and authority of the Scriptures, the "big picture" of the Bible, how to teach interactively, etc. Designed for use by teachers, it is not really suited for self-study.

• *House Church Weekend Workshops* — NTRF teams are available to conduct weekend workshops on God's design for His church. For more information, contact us through the web site NTRF.ORG. There is no charge for our teaching ministry.

• *Traditions* — A six tape audio cassette series by London house church elder Beresford Job that traces the rise of many church traditions common today that actually have no basis in the Scriptures, and that often times go directly against the commands of God.

• *Financing The Work* — An audio cassette dealing with what the NT says about supporting church workers (such as evangelists, apostles, & elders). Concerns how to, who, why, etc.

• *How To Teach Interactively* — An audio cassette & handout on how to lead an interactive Bible study (the method Jesus used with small groups).

• *Annual Southern House Church Conference Tapes* — Cassette tapes from last year's keynote speaker's plenary sessions.

Many of our resources can be downloaded directly off the internet.

WWW.NTRF.ORG

new testament
restoration
foundation